P9-DCH-598

THE YESTERMORROW CLOTHES BOOK

Drawings by
CECILIE STARIN
Julia Gombert

Photos by
Suzanne M. Nyerges
Neal Brisker
Richard Ruthsatz

Chilton Book Company / Radnor, Pennsylvania

THE YESTERMORROW CLOTHES BOOK

How to Remodel Secondhand Clothes

DIANA FUNARO

Copyright © 1976 by Diana Funaro

All Rights Reserved

Published in Radnor, Pa., by Chilton Book Company
and simultaneously in Don Mills, Ont., Canada
by Thomas Nelson & Sons, Ltd.

Manufactured in the United States of America
Designed by Arlene Putterman

LIBRARY OF CONGRESS CATALOGING IN PUBLICATION DATA
Funaro, Diana.
    The yestermorrow clothes book.

    Bibliography: p. 160
    Includes index.
    1. Clothing and dress. 2. Tailoring. 3. Tailoring
(Women's) I. Title.
TT560.F86 1976   646.4'04   76-26636
ISBN 0-8019-6407-5
ISBN 0-8019-6408-3 pbk.

Fashion renderings by Enrico Sacchetti from his *Robes et femmes*, 1913,
reprinted by courtesy of the publisher, Dorbon-Aîné, Tours, France.
From the collection of Bruce Chilton Lane.

Cover photograph, interior of *Harold's Place*, by Suzanne M. Nyerges.
Shown standing, from left, Leslie Pagett and Nina Anthony Reneka;
seated, Suzanne Horton. Clothing courtesy of *Harold's Place*.
Author photograph, back flap, by Suzanne M. Nyerges.

2 3 4 5 6 7 8 9 0   5 4 3 2 1 0 9 8 7

ACKNOWLEDGMENTS

Special thanks to Cheryl Purdue for bringing her dynamic yet mellow Big Sur energy to the project, and for her assistance with the research and contributions to the sewing instructions.

Thanks also to Tami Lane, who worked with me in the early stages and for her careful proofreading of the manuscript and pages.

My appreciation to these talented young designers for their imaginative remodeling ideas: Laurie Hazlett, J. J. Smith, and Mary McCrea.

To my editor, Benton Arnovitz, for his diligent discretion, and to Kathy Conover for meticulous copy editing. Thanks also to Glen Ruh for his total support. To Edna Jones, Elsie Comninos, and the entire Chilton Book Company staff.

For the use of their clothes in the photographs, my appreciation to Melodie, Bob, and John of *The Crystal Palace*, West Hollywood; Terry and B. J. of *Charlotte's Web*, Studio City; and Caroline of *The Dusty Ruffle*, Topanga.

For the use of clothes and the interior of their shop for the cover photograph, thanks to Diana, Tara, and Harold of *Harold's Place*, Beverly Hills.

To Lisa Morriss for supplying valuable information for the cleaning section, making available her museum knowledge of textile conservation. And to the helpful librarians of the Los Angeles County Museum of Art.

To Rande Lisle, designer and illustrator, for helping to develop the format for the drawings.

Thanks to our roving Yestermorrow correspondents overseas: Fran Funaro and Colin Murchi.

To Barry Haldeman and Alan Wertheimer for their legal wizardry, and to Rochelle Pollack for keeping it all smooth.

For help in various forms, many thanks to: Donna and Russel of *Donna's Antique Clothing Store,* Hollywood; Jintz, Suzanne Horton, Linda Melin, Margie Craig, Tom Vinetz, Art Hill, Fred Havens, Stephanie Lipney, Charlene Scott, Mary Funaro Webb, Meg Geiss, Sylvia Lane Winner, Chris Zuback, Rosina Kroner, Christalene, Lauren Pillsbury, Patti Nast, Robert Mann, Penny Gottlieb, Jim Elyea, Paul Greenstein, Sue Wong, Helen Herbert, Celia Kaye, Nonyia Finklestein, Judy Morris, August Agustsson, Terry Forgette, Mary Arutunian, Vic and Shirley Henderson, Christene Campbell, Corinne Dromard, Paul Camen, Bob Seidemann, and to all the antique clothes aficionados of LA.

Extra special thanks to Bruce Chilton Lane, who was there before the beginning and who helped in every phase of the project.

A loving thanks to two special people in my world, Anna and Anthony Funaro.

CONTENTS

x

INTRODUCTION

Among the wide variety of clothes styles available from the 1900s to the 1940s, you can find casual wool sweaters, delicate lace petticoats, and sultry Harlow gowns. The fabrics often have one-of-a-kind prints and unusual, muted colors. Generally, these old garments were constructed with more care and attention to detail than is usual nowadays. But perhaps the best part is that with just a little searching you can find treasures like these for only a few dollars.

The condition of these old clothes varies, of course, depending mainly on where they're found and how old they are. Some can be worn as is. Others will need fit and style changes or repairs. Secondhand clothes are very adaptable, though, and needn't look period or even old. A practical approach is to mix a few choice old pieces, a '40s fake fur for example, with clothes you already have. A friend recently found an old silk kimono robe with a damaged hem at the Rose Bowl Swap Meet for one dollar. She cut the kimono off at the hips, tied it around her waist, and now wears it as a colorful, lightweight top for jeans.

Marvelous bargains like this can be found at thrift shops, garage sales, swap meets, estate sales, or secondhand clothing boutiques. The Salvation Army and Goodwill Industries are just two of the well-known nationwide outfits which operate thrift shops that carry secondhand clothes. Others are run by The Association of Junior Leagues, Hadassah, and St. Vincent de Paul. Check the Yellow Pages for these and other local secondhand or thrift shops. Also, look through the classified sections of your local newspapers and magazines for announcements of garage and estate sales. And don't forget the hidden treasures in your own attic, cellar, or garage.

There are many good costume history books which can give you specifics on style changes over the decades. James Laver has written several excellent books on the subject. One good survey is *The Concise History of Costume and Fashion,* which is probably available at your library. Old sewing books and fashion magazines, *Vogue* or *Harper's* for instance, are fun to look through for ideas and inspiration, and can often be found at used book and magazine shops. A very personal costume history, though, can be found in your own family photograph albums. Perhaps you'll spot Mom and Dad in their forties fineries or Grandma in her high-neck lace wedding dress.

You can get an endless source of fashion ideas from old films—and they're such a treat to watch. The other night I saw one of Harry Houdini's silent films. It had plenty of predictable tie-up and escape scenes, but the parts I found particularly fascinating were the closeups of those tiny toque hats that I had read about but never seen. They were embellished with long, bird-of-paradise plumes that stood straight up. In films like these you not only see the fashions and makeup, but also the spirit and sensibilities behind the styles.

The clothes shown in this book are a sampling of those found at various thrift shops and garage sales. Since one of the virtues of old clothing is its uniqueness, each item different from the next, the remodeling ideas aren't all meant to be followed literally. Instead they're intended as examples of the kinds of changes possible—to stimulate your own creative thinking.

The instructions are for those who have some experience with sewing. But the remodeling ideas don't require an intimate knowledge of clothing construction, since that was done for you years ago. Simple changes can be made on specific features of the garment, perhaps at the waist or shoulders, allowing you to drastically alter the style or fit. If shoulders are drooping, for example, you can insert shoulder pads with a few simple stitches. Or if a dress is boxy and long, it can be brought in and up with merely a belt.

Before you begin any project, however, it's important to read over the instructions first. You probably already have most of the tools you'll need—scissors, needles, pins, and thread. One of the most important tools for working with fragile old clothes is a seam ripper. When other types of tools are needed for special fabrics, such as delicate lingerie or knits, they are listed at the beginning of appropriate sections.

Finally, in the process of transforming these valuable old clothes, I hope that you will find among them the classic elements that span yesterday and tomorrow.

2

1 /
CLEANING
AND
FRESHENING

Wouldn't it be convenient if all the old clothes you found were spotless, sweet-smelling, and otherwise in ready-to-wear condition? The fact is, however, that you'll probably have to clean or at least freshen most old garments you come across. Each item can present a different cleaning problem depending upon its condition, fabric, and ornamentation. And there are times when a professional knowledge of textiles, dyes, and chemicals is required before you can proceed. But don't get discouraged: here are some general guide-lines you can follow. If you're uncertain, better ask your local dry cleaners for help.

FABRIC IDENTIFICATION

Before you attempt to clean your garment, you need to know the kind of fabric it's made of. Some fabrics can be washed; others need to be dry cleaned. Unfortunately, you may have problems identifying the fabric since clothes made before the '60s don't usually have fabric content and cleaning instruction labels attached. There were relatively few fibers used before the '50s compared to what's available today. Basically these were natural fibers—cotton, linen, wool, and silk. Rayon came into general use around the turn of the century, acetate in the mid-20s.

Natural fibers are generally familiar and recognizable, but rayon and acetate can be made to resemble these fibers. To eliminate confusion, you can try a burn test. Make this test by first pulling a thread or two from a seam or the hem of your garment. Then burn the threads with a match. Fibers will burn in different ways, producing distinctive odors and residues. Check your results with the Burn Test chart.

Burn Test

FIBER	BURNS	ODOR	RESIDUE
Cotton	Rapidly, with steady leaping flame—faster than linen	Burning paper	Light, feathery gray ash
Linen	Slower than cotton, leaping flame	Burning paper	Same ash as cotton
Wool	Slower than pure silk, sputters	Burning hair	Brittle beads, easily crushed
Silk (pure)	Slowly, with sputters	Burning hair	Brittle beads, easily crushed
Silk (weighted)	Slowly, with sputters	Burning hair, metallic	Screenlike skeleton of fiber
Rayon	Rapidly, as cotton	Burning paper	Soft gray ash, practically none
Acetate	Rapidly, sputters and melts	Hot vinegar	Shiny black beads, not easily crushed
Nylon	Without flame, melts and drips	Boiling celery	Hard gray or black beads

If you still can't figure out what the fabric is after this test, take the garment to a dry cleaner or a large fabric shop. Professionals there should be able to make a positive identification.

PREPARATION FOR CLEANING

Before proceeding to either wash or dry clean, here are some preliminary things you can do for better results.

Old, delicate, or fancy trimmings such as lace may tear and should be removed before cleaning. Also remove shoulder pads and wash them separately, if washable.

Remove any metal trims or fastenings that are rusted or broken, such as hooks and eyes or glass buttons. Close zippers.

If there are beads, check to see if they are secure. Often old beads were sewn on with a chain stitch that easily unravels once the thread is broken. If this has happened, resew the beads or remove them until after cleaning. Another hint is to sew strips of net over beaded areas to protect them.

Measure knits or other loosely woven fabrics before cleaning. This way you can block a garment back into its original shape.

If the garment is very dusty or has a lot of loose dirt, vacuum or brush it. Use a small, low-powered hand vacuum cleaner, not the large one you use to clean carpets. On such sturdy items as overcoats, simply move the vacuum back and forth a few inches above the garment. For more delicate fabrics, place a sheet of nylon or fiberglass screening on top before vacuuming. Do not attempt to vacuum torn areas or lightweight fabrics because the suction can tear them.

If you don't have a small vacuum, hang the garment outside and brush it with a good watercolor or housepaint brush made of natural bristles.

HANDLING WASHABLES

When you know the kind of fabric, you can decide how an item should be cleaned. Old cotton and linen that are colorfast can usually be washed, preferably by hand; old silk, wool, rayon, and acetate should be dry cleaned. Wool sweaters can be washed by hand; see the cleaning and blocking information in Chapter 7.

Stains

Most standard stain-removal techniques recommended today won't work on old clothes because the best time to remove a stain is when it first happens. Old stains have undergone chemical changes and have become set and permanent because of age and heat. Your chances of getting stains removed from old garments are slim, so consider this before buying a stain-ridden item.

Of course, you can always decorate over stains using embroidery, beading, applique, or lace. Be creative with your designs: perhaps make connecting patterns of embroidery so that the effect looks complete; or try dyeing the entire garment a darker color. See Chapter 3 for more ideas on decorative camouflage.

Color Fastness

Your old clothing should be tested for color fastness before being either washed or dry cleaned. Otherwise, running of the dye or bleeding can occur, ruining your one-of-a-kind garment. Each color must be tested separately. It is important to remember that even though a garment looks entirely one color, two or more fabrics with different dyes may have been used. Check carefully; if this is the case, test each fabric separately. The same rule applies to various trimmings, such as applique: isolate trim from the fabric and test for color fastness.

If your garment is going to be dry cleaned, instruct the cleaner to test for color fastness beforehand with the different solutions he will be using in the cleaning.

If you determine that a fabric is washable, test it first in all the solutions you'll be using in the laundering process. This means you will need three containers: one with plain water; one with a solution of glycerin and water (recommended as a soil emulsifier in the washing process in the following section); and one with soap and water.

Place a white towel or cloth under the garment and drop a small amount of plain water on an inconspicuous part—use an eye dropper if you have one. Then gently rub a

5

Q-tip over the test area. If it picks up any dye color, or if the cloth under the garment has any dye on it, don't attempt to wash it. Send it instead to the dry cleaner. (Don't be misled by discoloration resulting from dirt.) If there is no dye bleeding, continue testing in this manner with the other solutions, checking for dye after each application. When you find there is still no dye bleeding after all the colors and fabrics of the garment have been tested, go ahead and wash.

Soaking

If your garment is heavily soiled, you may want to soak it in a solution of glycerin and water before washing. Glycerin acts as an emulsifier, loosening ground-in dirt, and can be bought at most drugstores. The solution is mixed with one part glycerin to four parts lukewarm water (about 90° F). If the solution becomes murky with dirt, change it and resoak the garment until the water remains clear. But don't soak it too long—some professionals say not more than ten minutes—because dirt can become retrapped within the fabric.

Hand Washing

It's best to wash old clothes by hand rather than in a machine. Even though signs of age may not be visible on a garment, the fibers could be weak enough to break from the agitation of a washing machine.

Very delicate garments, for example, a Victorian lace blouse, will require even more care. Fine pieces can be washed in net bags designed for washing hosiery. Or you can place the garment between two layers of soft net, then sew the net together using a running stitch every few inches. If there are torn areas or holes, sew the entire edge of the hole to the net to prevent further damage.

Wash the garment in a lukewarm (90° F) to cool soap and water solution. Make sure the water is not hot—heat weakens fibers and fades colors. Soft water is preferred, since the minerals in hard water can harm fibers, as well as give them a stiff feeling and an unpleasant odor. You can buy packaged water softeners at the supermarket which are added, like soap, to your wash water. Use a small amount of a neutral soap—one with a balanced pH so that it is not excessively alkaline or acidic. Neutrogena and Joy are good brands commonly available.

Another good cleaning agent is called Orvus. It is one of the most neutral of soaps and is used by museums in the conservation of antique clothes. Indeed, it is so mild that it is also used by veterinarians to bathe dogs. Orvus can be purchased at dry-cleaning supply stores or where veterinary supplies are sold. The soap is usually available only in large quantities—a gallon minimum. It is a concentrate, so you will only need a little of the soft paste to get a sinkful of suds.

Don't rub soap directly onto the fabric. Start with thick suds, best prepared by running hot water onto the soap flakes or liquid until dissolved, then letting it cool down to the desired temperature. Gently squeeze the suds through the garment; *do not wring or twist*. If the garment is very soiled, use a second sudsing when the water becomes dark.

6

Rinsing

Rinse the garment several times, in the same temperature water in which it was washed, until the water is clear and there is no soap smell left. Don't allow water to come spraying out from the tap directly onto the fabric—the weight of the water may cause damage.

After thoroughly rinsing, blot excess water out gently with clean towels. Don't wring or twist the fabric; this is too hard on old fibers. If you're dissatisfied with the appearance of the garment, repeat the washing process.

Drying

Natural drying is best. Even though some electric dryers have a "no heat" setting, the thermostat may be inaccurate and should not be trusted. Only very sturdy garments should be put in the dryer. On the other hand, hanging garments that are wet may cause stretching and produce unwanted strain on the shoulders. It's better to lay the garment out flat, just as you would a good hand-washed sweater.

You can dry the garment outdoors by laying it on a fresh dry towel, out of direct sunlight. Indoors, the garment can be dried on a towel or, preferably, on a screen specially designed for this purpose and available at most department stores. Drying screens are normally suspended horizontally across a bathtub.

Bleaching

If, after washing and partial drying, you can tell that your white cotton or linen garment is still stained or yellowed, you may *cautiously* try whitening it with bleach. You need to be extremely careful because bleach can radically deteriorate weak cotton and linen fibers. Some bleaches are longer lasting in their whitening effect than others. The two methods described here include lemon juice and sodium perborate—a mild and long-lasting bleach.

Lemon juice is one of the oldest known bleaching agents, a method handed down from mother to daughter for generations. Place the washed, still wet garment in a nonmetal container filled with a solution of soap, hot tap water cooled to lukewarm, and about one tablespoonful of lemon juice per gallon of water.

After soaking, dry the garment outside in direct sunlight on a towel, perhaps over plastic. If the garment dries before the desired amount of whiteness is attained, bleach again. Then rewash it and follow the drying suggestions discussed in the previous section. It is important that temperature changes be gradual—no extremes. If you live in a cold climate, use this technique only in the spring or summer months.

A second bleaching method uses sodium perborate, an active ingredient in many commercial bleaches, such as Snowy and Clorox 2. Fill a nonmetal sink with hot tap water, soap suds, and a small amount of bleach—about one tablespoonful of sodium perborate to a gallon of water. Let the water cool to lukewarm before inserting the garment. Never use a large amount of bleach; instead, repeat the process using one tablespoonful of bleach each time.

Place the washed, still wet item in the solution. Let it soak, checking frequently until the desired whiteness is attained. Then rinse in cool water repeatedly until the water is clear and no bleach odor remains. Dry as described above.

DRY CLEANING

If your garment is silk, wool, rayon, or acetate, dry cleaning is recommended. Before you proceed, there are several things you should be aware of.

Professional

Some cleaners are hesitant to clean fragile old things because the clothes may not withstand the vigorous cleaning procedure. Even with special hand treatment, requiring a lot of time and attention (and a lot of your money), a cleaner may not be able to guarantee the results. Try to find a large, well-established business that has had a lot of experience with various garments, old and new. Then be sure to have them pretest for color fastness and remove any special trims (see Preparation for Cleaning).

A brief look at the general dry-cleaning procedure may help alert you to the various risks involved. First, items are classified by color and fabric into large loads (machines can hold up to 500 pounds). The load is then dropped into a basket which in turn is put into a large, solvent-filled machine. The garments are then rubbed against each other, the sides of the basket, and the solvent, producing the necessary friction to clean them. The solvent is then extracted by means of centrifugal force. All these mechanical actions can cause a brittle or rigid old fabric to break. The drying time and temperatures are determined by the kind of solvent used and the fabric involved. Proper classification of the loads is imperative, as a wrong decision can cause shrinkage, wrinkling, or splitting.

Coin Operated

If you believe your garment is sturdy enough to withstand the agitation of the dry-cleaning process, try using the self-service, coin-operated dry-cleaning machines. They're economical when you have a number of things to clean at once, since it costs only about three dollars to clean up to eight pounds. Doing it this way also saves time. The clothes can be cleaned and ready to go in an hour. Instructions are posted and professionals are on hand if you need additional advice.

Here are some points to remember:

Before using any stain removal solvents, first test them on an inconspicuous spot to be sure they won't remove any dye.

To remove wrinkling, bring the clothes in on padded hangers and rehang them as soon as they come from the machine.

Separate light from dark, and heavily soiled from lightly soiled items.

Put more fragile items into a mesh bag or pillowcase.

Don't dry clean plastic, rubber, fur, leather, or feathers.

Cleaning and Freshening

PRESSING

Don't confuse ironing with pressing. Ironing is pushing the weight of the iron down and sliding it over the fabric. Pressing is lifting and lowering the iron lightly onto each area of the garment, following the straight of grain. The weight of the iron is kept in your hand, not placed on the fabric. This retains the shape of the garment and saves the fabric finish. Pressing is obviously the gentler method and the one that should be used on your old clothes.

Generally, it's best to press on the wrong side of the garment using the steam setting on your iron. Steam provides added moisture to help remove wrinkles and gives a more professional look. A damp, *not* wet, pressing cloth or towel placed between the garment and the iron will give even more moisture. If you're pressing on the right side, a pressing cloth is a must to protect the garment from scorches, spit marks, and shine.

Before you begin to press make sure your ironing board has a smooth, padded surface and that the bottom of your iron is clean. Also keep the fabric in mind when pressing; change the heat and the amount of moisture used accordingly. Too much heat or moisture, leaving the iron in one place too long, and pressing too frequently can give an overpressed look. Specific hints for pressing certain fabrics follow.

Lightweight Cotton, Silk, Rayon, Other Manmades. Use low heat and a damp pressing cloth if you need extra moisture; press on the wrong side to eliminate shine. Be careful with silk, as a too-hot iron can weaken and sometimes discolor it. It can also water spot, so use very little moisture.

Wool. Use moist heat. Do not press wool when it is totally wet or dry: when wet it will shrink; when dry it cannot be shaped as well. While it is slightly damp from the steam of the iron, brush it with a clothesbrush to raise the nap.

Heavy Cotton and Linen. Use a higher heat. Use a pressing cloth to eliminate shine on dark colors. Linen may need more moisture, so dampen the pressing cloth.

Velvets, Corduroys, Other Napped Fabrics. Press on the wrong side over a needle board (a board covered with soft fine wires, available in notions departments), or a self-fabric pressing cloth. If the garment isn't too fragile, steam it over a tub of hot water, checking every so often to be sure no water drops form on the fabric. Let it hang until thoroughly dry. Try not to handle these fabrics when they're still damp because you can leave fingermarks. Gently brush the finish of the garment when dry. Flattened pile cannot be restored.

Laces and Veilings. "Press" with steam instead of with pressure. Do this by moving a steam iron back and forth just above the fabric. Don't let the iron rest directly on it.

Bias Fabrics. Press in the direction of the *straight* of grain to prevent unwanted stretching.

FRESHENING WITH HERBS

Treasures taken from attics or trunks often have an unmistakably musty odor. Also, some old clothes may reek of mothballs. A simple but effective answer is to hang them on padded hangers, lessening strain on the shoulders, and put them outside to air. Keep

9

colored garments out of direct sunlight so no fading occurs. The freshening process can continue indoors, using fragrant potpourris and pomander balls in your drawers and closets.

Potpourris

Potpourris are mixtures of dried flower petals and spices that can be made into sachets. The ingredients are available at herb stores (check the Yellow Pages under *Herbs*) and fall into three groups: flower petals or herb leaves for bulk; spices or essential oils for scent; and special fixative herbs to make the scent last longer.

Make your own blend by choosing your favorite flower petals or herb leaves as a base. Put them in a glass or enamel bowl and use a wooden spoon. (Don't use any metal.) Scent them with some fragrant spices like cloves, a little dried orange peel, or a few drops of some exotic essential oil, such as jasmine—essential oils have no alcohol added and are used as bases for perfumes. Then add a powdered fixative, for example, orris root or calamus (about ½ ounce to a quart of petals) to hold the scent. Store in covered jars for a month or two so the fragrances blend. Stuff small fabric bags with the blend, making sure the spices and fixatives are evenly distributed between each bag. Here are instructions for making two aromatic potpourris.

ROSE AND SPICE
1 quart crisply dried rose petals
1 cup lavender flowers
½ cup orris root, crushed
1 tsp. ground mace
1 tsp. crushed cinnamon stick
1 tbsp. cardamon seeds, crushed
5 drops oil of rose

HERB AND SPICE
½ cup dried lemon peel
½ cup dried orange peel
2 cups marjoram leaves
2 cups rosemary leaves
1 cup sage leaves
1 ounce orris root, crushed
1 tbsp. ground cloves
5 drops oil of lemon or orange

Pomander Balls

Pomander balls are oranges studded with whole cloves. They are very fragrant when dried and are a perfect freshener for closets. They have the added advantage of keeping moths away—moths hate cloves. You can make pomander balls using large, firm oranges. Stick whole cloves into the orange until the peel is completely covered with them.

To make this easier you can first pierce the orange peel with a fork or skewer. Then roll the orange in a mixture of equal parts (1½–2 tablespoons) of powdered cinnamon, cloves, mace, and orris root or calamus (fixatives). Pat the powder in so it adheres to the orange and then wrap the fruit in tissue paper.

Put the orange in a cupboard or other dry place for about two weeks. As it dries the orange will shrink and the spicy fragrance will emerge. When it has completely dried remove the tissue paper, shake off any loose powder, and tie a ribbon around it. Hang the pomander in your closet. The fragrance should keep for years.

Herbal Moth Repellents

A pleasant substitute for the standard camphor mothballs are moth-repellent herbs. These herbs can be mixed together, sewn into small cloth bags, and placed among your woolens or furs. The fragrance is fresh and woodsy.

Choose from among the following herbs and add some orris root or calamus for preservation. You can add a few cloves, which also give a nice spicy scent, as an extra moth chaser.

MOTH-REPELLENT HERBS
rosemary
southernwood
pennyroyal
wormwood
bay leaves
cedar wood
sassafras

Here's an effective moth-repellent recipe that includes essential oil of rosemary:

ROSEMARY AND HERBS
1 cup rosemary
1 cup cedarwood
1 cup southernwood
2 tbsp. cloves
2 or 3 drops oil of rosemary

12

13

2 /
MENDING

Years ago, mending was considered an art and many elaborate techniques were used, especially during the two world wars and the depression. Hours were spent carefully repairing stockings, linens, or lace with the objective of making all repairs as invisible as possible. Worn threads were reinforced using intricate handweaving or darning techniques that required skillful needlework, lots of patience, and 20–20 vision. Many kinds of invisible patches were used, such as the overhand, round underlaid, fitted, or tailored, using excess fabric from hems or facings. The kind of mending done today is much less extensive—often limited to replacing buttons or a zipper.

In this chapter there are some simple suggestions for repairing common trouble spots, such as small holes, ripped underarms and seams, or frayed edges. But before you begin to mend an old garment be sure the item is strong enough to make the effort worthwhile; if the fabric is too weak it can fall apart soon after it's fixed. Test the item by pulling gently on the fabric to be sure it won't rip under this slight strain, or hold the garment up to a bright light to be sure the fibers aren't worn thin.

HOLES AND TEARS

If your garment has a tiny hole or tear, it can be mended by simply stitching the edges together on the wrong side as you would a seam. If there's a slit in the fabric and you don't want to seam the edges, use a zigzag stitch to make a type of darn. Press the area first and trim away any loose threads or uneven edges. Put a backing fabric underneath and pin the edges of the slit to it so they meet. Zigzag over the slit, extending the stitches beyond the ends of the tear. Trim the backing close to the stitching line.

If the damage is in an area of your garment the machine can't reach, sew it together by hand using tiny running or overcast stitches. Don't draw the stitches up too tightly. There must be give so the thread won't break. Extend the stitching beyond the ends of the tear and fasten the threads at each end.

If the damaged area of your garment is too large to mend in the above ways, use a reinforcement patch on the underside to add strength; then cover it using the decorative ideas in Chapter 3. The reinforcement patch should be made of strong, soft, pliable fabric. You should be able to clean it the same way you plan to clean the garment. Cut the patch so it extends at least 1 inch beyond the damaged area. Finish the patch edges by hemming or zigzagging them, then pin it to the garment with wrong sides together. Stitch it on, using either a straight or zigzag stitch.

RIPPED UNDERARMS

One way to repair a ripped underarm is to insert a gusset. A gusset is a form of patch cut on the bias to give maximum stretch so you can move freely without tearing the garment. In fact, gussets slightly increase the size of the garment because of the added material. For this reason, insert them at both underarms so the garment will be even on both sides. Gussets are usually cut in either triangular or diamond shapes. If the entire armhole is ripped, including sleeve and body, use a diamond-shaped gusset, as shown in Figure 1. The triangular shape is used if your garment is sleeveless or if just the body portion is ripped. See the instructions below for this type of gusset. Use fabric that's as close to that of your garment as you can find. Double it if the fabric is sheer so it will be strong enough.

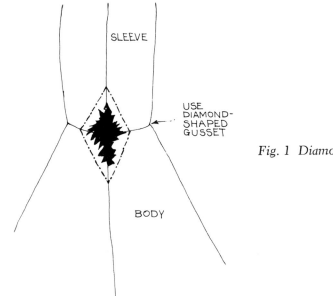

Fig. 1 Diamond-shaped gusset

INSERTING A TRIANGULAR GUSSET

1. Undo the sleeve a little on both sides of the side seam. Neatly trim around the tear, making a V shape as shown in Figure 2. Measure the V and make the gusset the same size, plus ½ inch for seam allowances.

2. Cut out the gusset on the bias of the fabric so that it will have give—that is, cut on the diagonal of the lengthwise and crosswise threads.

3. Reinforce the point of the V if you like, using 14–18 stitches per inch, and stitch ⅛ inch from the edge, taking one stitch at the point.

4. With wrong sides facing up, pin the gusset to the edges of the V, right sides together. Stitch as in step 3 above.

5. Press the seams toward the garment, away from the gusset. You can topstitch on the outside of the garment close to the seamline if you want reinforcement. Then resew the sleeve to the garment (Figure 3).

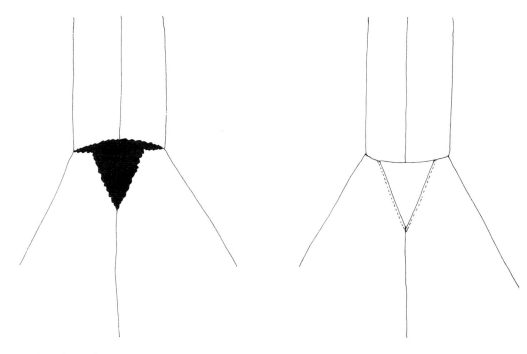

Fig. 2 Edges of triangular tear are trimmed   *Fig. 3 Topstitched triangular gusset*

RIPPED SEAMS

Ripped seams can be the result of simple wear and tear, worn thread, or stitching that's too tight. Before you restitch, make sure the tension of your machine is right for the fabric—that is, more tension for heavy fabrics, less for lightweight ones. Also check the stitch length so it is appropriate for the fabric. Then clip and remove all broken threads; resew the seam with a strong, somewhat stretchy thread like a cotton-polyester blend. You can pull the fabric slightly as you sew to incorporate stretch into the seam or, if you're sewing on sweaters or knits, use a zigzag stitch for more stretch. If the seam is overcast, lapped, or flat felled, undo the stitching beyond the break so it is easier to redo.   19

Then match the new seam stitching to the original as best you can. (See Chapter 9 for details on lapped and flat-felled seams.) If the seams are undone in an area the machine can't reach, such as in corners, folds, or where two seams meet, stitch by hand: use tiny backstitches and fasten the threads at each end.

In cases where the fabric rather than the stitching has pulled apart at a seam, the garment was probably too tight or the fabric too loosely woven. Depending upon how the garment fits you, either take the seam in, so the stitching is now on the seam allowance, or let it out. If this leaves a too-narrow seam allowance, sew seam binding to the edges. Then cover the worn part with decorative trims of ribbons or fabric bands. You can try to blend the color of the trim with that of the garment or contrast it and repeat it elsewhere, perhaps outlining other structural borders.

WORN CLOSURES

Because zippers weren't used widely until the late '30s, garments made before that time were closed with buttons, hooks and eyes, or snaps. If your old garments have these closures you may need to mend, resew, or strengthen them. Or you could replace them with a zipper.

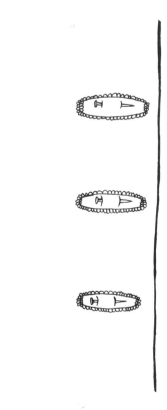

20   *Fig. 4 Mixed buttons produce eclectic look*   *Fig. 5 Marking placement for buttons*

Mending

Buttons

If any buttons are missing you can replace all of them with another set of old or new buttons. You can also purchase metal clasps for covered buttons in any notions department: make your own covered buttons with matching fabric from garment hem or excess from seams. Or, instead of buying anything, add various shaped buttons to mix with the existing ones for a different look as shown in Figure 4. To get the right size buttons, measure the thickness as well as the diameter of an original button.

To ascertain correct placement for the buttons you're sewing on, lap the buttonhole side of the closure over the button side. Put a pin through the buttonhole and secure it on the bottom layer where the button should be (Figure 5). Then sew the buttons on at each pin so they will be aligned properly and the closure will be flat and smooth. When you sew buttons on, use strong thread like buttonhole twist. Don't sew buttons down too tightly; you need to allow room for the buttonhole fabric underneath. If the button doesn't have a shank, make one by wrapping the thread around the stitching between the button and the garment, as shown in Figure 6.

Fig. 6 Wrapped thread creates shank between button and fabric

If a button has pulled off leaving a small hole, zigzag stitch a patch of strong fabric over it on the underside. Then resew the button. If the torn area is large and shows beyond the buttonhole, sew a double band of fabric or trim down the entire button side of the closure. Then cut away the original fabric from underneath and sew buttons onto the new band.

Buttonholes

If there are tiny rips or frays at the edge of a buttonhole, stitch around them using a hand or machine buttonhole stitch and matching thread. Or sew the buttonholes closed from the wrong side, then cover them with a band of fabric or other trim. Sew snaps to the underside of the old buttonholes and replace the buttons with the other halves of the snaps (Figure 7).

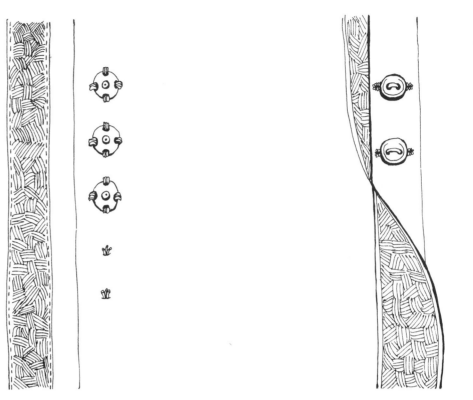

Fig. 7 *Worn buttonholes are covered and*
snaps added for closure

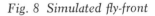

Fig. 8 *Simulated fly-front*

You can make a simulated fly-front by sewing fabric or trimming over the button-hole edge, attaching it only along the inside edge. Then close the buttons underneath the fabric or trim, as shown in Figure 8. You can also sew up worn buttonholes, replace the buttons, and cover them with Oriental frog closures, as shown in Figure 9.

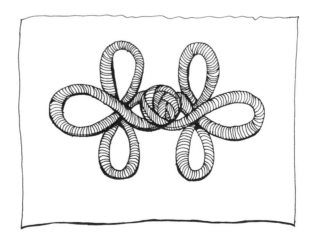

Fig. 9 *Oriental frog closures*
replace worn buttonholes

Hooks and Eyes and Snaps

Make sure hooks and eyes or snaps are placed close enough together so there aren't any gaps in the closure. Also be sure the opposing parts of the fasteners are directly aligned so the closure will be even and lie flat. Stitch hooks and eyes and snaps as shown in Figure 10.

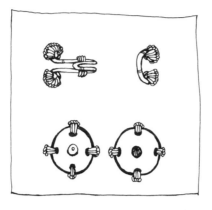

Fig. 10 Stitching snaps and hooks and eyes

Zippers

You may want to replace the old fastenings, such as hooks and eyes, or snaps, with a zipper. The instructions here are for the lapped method, which can be used at the side or center back of a garment—instructions are illustrated for a side insertion on a dress. The lapped method is particularly good for old clothing because it conceals the zipper more than the centered type; thus, it is helpful when you're having trouble matching the color of a new zipper to that of an old dress. Buy a zipper as close to the length of the side opening as possible, matching the color as best you can, then proceed as follows.

PREPARING THE GARMENT

1. Remove the old fastenings with a seam ripper, being careful not to tear the fabric.

2. Press the zipper tape flat and line the zipper up with the opening. Mark the distance between the zipper stops on the opening with pins. If the existing opening is shorter or longer than the distance between the pins, adjust it by letting it out or sewing it closed so it lines up exactly with the pins (Figure 11).

3. Measure the width of the seam allowance in the side opening. It should be no less than ½ inch to sew the zipper on properly. If it is less you will have to sew seam binding onto the raw edges to widen it. Do this by pinning the binding to the top of the seam allowance, extending its length 1 inch to either side of the pins. Then sew the binding to the allowance with a hand hemming stitch or a machine topstitch (Figure 12). Remove all the pins.

23

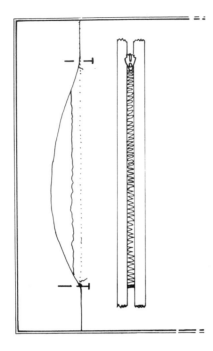

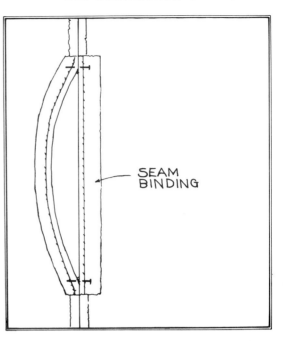

SEAM
BINDING

Fig. 11 *Zipper stops are aligned with garment opening*

Fig. 12 *Binding increases width of seam allowance*

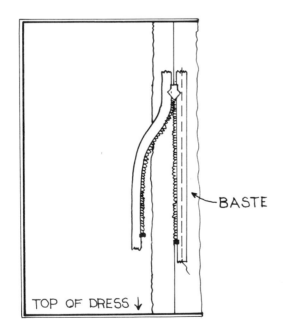

BASTE

TOP OF DRESS ↓

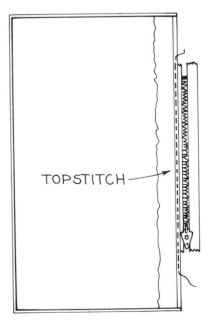

TOPSTITCH—

Fig. 13 *Machine baste zipper, working from bottom to top*

Fig. 14 *Topstitching through fabric and zipper tape*

INSERTING ZIPPER IN SIDE OF DRESS

1. Baste the zipper opening closed. Press seam allowances open.

2. Remove the presser foot from the machine and attach a zipper foot.

3. Turn the dress wrong side out with the top of the garment facing down—the dress is upside down. Smooth the fabric under the zipper opening to the left so that the right seam allowance (seam allowance on back of dress) is extended.

4. Place the zipper face down and opened on the extended seam allowance. The top and bottom stops of the zipper should meet the ends of the temporary basting stitches, and the zipper teeth should be placed on the seamline. With the zipper foot to the right of the needle, baste the zipper to the extended seam allowance (Figure 13). Work from the bottom to the top of the zipper.

5. Close the zipper and turn it face up. Smooth the fabric away from the zipper teeth to the left. Move the zipper foot to the left and, with regular length stitches, top-stitch through the folded seam allowance (Figure 14). Again, work from the bottom to the top of zipper.

6. Place the garment flattened out, the zipper face down. Stitch across the bottom edge of the zipper just outside the stop, up the left side, and across the top (Figure 15). Remove the basting stitches that are holding the seam closed and press.

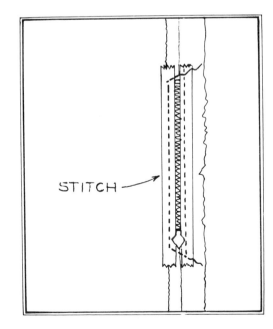

*Fig. 15 Zipper tape is stitched across
bottom, up left side, and across the top*

FRAYED AND STAINED EDGES

Frayed and stained edges usually occur at hems and cuffs. Four solutions are proposed below.

A quick way to cover damage is to use trims, fabric bands, or decorative stitching, then repeat the trim elsewhere on the garment for a coordinated look.

If there is ample length, you can undo the hem and turn the damaged edge under so it doesn't show. Then restitch the hem.

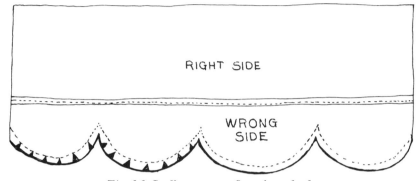

RIGHT SIDE

WRONG SIDE

Fig. 16 Scallops camouflage frayed edges

You can cut the damaged part off in a straight line close to the fold or make a scalloped edge as shown in Figure 16. Make a 2 inch facing and seam it to the cut edge. Then turn the facing to the inside and hem it to the garment.

Change the style of the garment by cutting above the damaged area. This way you can change long sleeves into short ones, a dress into a tunic top, or a floor-sweeping hem into a graceful, raised one as shown in Figure 17.

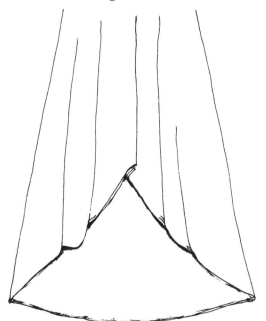

26   *Fig. 17 Raised hemline eliminates damaged fabric*

3 /
DECORATING

Decorative techniques can be used to camouflage irremovable stains, cover conspicuous mending, or just liven up a garment. They include patches, appliques, trims, embroidery, and dye. Whatever technique you use, be sure it's in harmony with the style and fabric of the garment. In other words, it should look like it belongs. Obviously, geometric patches won't look right on a long, flowing, lace dress and chiffon appliques won't work on a pair of jeans.

DECORATIVE PATCHES AND APPLIQUES

Decorative patches are usually geometric in shape, while appliques are often realistic or other kinds of designs. They can be purchased ready made or you can make them yourself. They can be used alone or in numbers to create a patchwork or collage effect. To make your own patches, cut fabrics into squares, rectangles, triangles, or diamonds. And to make appliques, use any shapes you like—common ones are flowers, birds, stars, and moons. Whatever shape you choose, it should be relatively simple and should suit the style of your garment.

The patch fabric can blend or contrast with the color and pattern of the garment. If the area you're patching is small, perhaps you can use fabric from a hem or seam allowance. If not, you'll have to find some other suitable fabric. But it should have the same cleaning characteristics as your garment (be careful of felt—it shrinks) and it should be strong. So if you use old fabric for patching check its strength before you sew

27

it on; if it's too weak it will tear shortly after it's worn. The weight of the patch fabric should be the same as the weight of the garment fabric or as close to it as possible. If you want to use a much lighter weight fabric, such as a lace patch on denim, back it with another, heavier fabric first. Commercial iron-on patches can be used, but they are stiff and heavy for light and medium-weight fabrics. Plus they often come undone around the edges after cleaning.

After you've chosen the fabric for the patches, measure the area you want to cover. Be sure to extend the patches a little beyond the damaged area. Draw or trace a design this size, plus ¼ inch for seam allowances, onto the patch fabric and cut it out. If you wish, you can mark the patch placement on the garment with tailor's chalk.

You can attach a patch or applique in one of two ways. The first is to pin or baste it to the garment and zigzag stitch it on with matching or contrasting thread. Stitch ¼ inch from the raw edge and go over the stitching a second time if the fabric ravels easily. Then trim the ¼ inch excess off as close to the stitching line as possible (Figure 18).

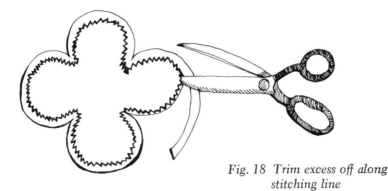

Fig. 18 *Trim excess off along stitching line*

This method of securing the patch with machine topstitching might not look right on lightweight, delicate fabrics. Also it may be difficult to do, as the edges of some sheer fabrics can fray when stitched by machine. If this is the case try the second method. This involves first pressing or basting under the ¼ inch allowance around the outside of the patch. (You can staystitch ¼ inch in from the edge first to make the hem turning easier if you like.) Then clip or notch curves and miter corners so you get a smooth, flat hem. Stitch the patch on by hand using a hemming or blanket stitch, or a slipstitch if you don't want the stitches to show. Don't pull the stitches too tightly or the fabric will pucker and the threads will break more easily.

Decorating

If you did not reinforce the damaged area prior to the decorative patching, cut the damage off close to the stitching line of the patch. You can give texture and dimension to the patch by filling it in with embroidery stitches, beads, quilting, or other trims. This filling in can be done before or after you sew the patch on to give more reinforcement to the area. Here are some patching variations.

Patchwork

Patchwork involves seaming together geometric-shaped patches. You can use a small bit of patchwork to fill in areas like yokes or bibs. Or make a larger piece of patchwork, using paper patterns, to make major garment sections like legs, skirts, and sleeves. The instructions here are for making a patchwork out of squares of the same size, cut from a variety of fabrics. These are then arranged so that the squares of fabric intermingle as shown in Figure 19.

Fig. 19 *Patchwork of identical-sized squares of different fabrics*

Fig. 20 *Wrong side of patchwork: seamed, clipped, pressed*

ASSEMBLING PATCHWORK

1. Measure the area where the patchwork will be placed and plan the patchwork for this size.

2. Make a paper pattern of the patch shape you want to use. Add ½ inch seam allowance on all sides of the pattern.

3. Using the paper pattern as a guide, cut as many patches as you need. Lay them out in the position in which they'll be sewn.

4. Stitch a horizontal row of patches together and press open the seam allowances. Do the same for the rest of the horizontal rows.

5. Stitch the sewn horizontal rows of patchwork together vertically and press the seam allowances open as shown in Figure 20.

31

32

Quilting

You can quilt patches, appliques, or patchwork for a deep, soft effect. Use cotton or Dacron batting or fiberfill for the padding. You can buy these at fabric shops or in large notions departments.

Cut the batting into the shape of your patch and place it between the patch and the garment or backing fabric. Stitch within the patch by hand or machine, making squares, diamonds, or other shapes (Figure 21). Do this either before or after the patch is attached to the garment.

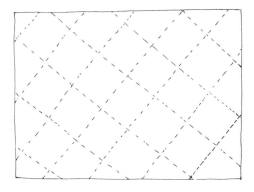

Fig. 21 Quilting stitches are usually done in geometric shapes—diamonds or squares

Collage

Appliques or decorative patches can be applied in collage form, that is, arranged in overlapping patterns and sewn on rather than seamed together as in patchwork.

Work your pattern out on paper first and pin the individual shapes to a light fabric backing. Zigzag stitch the edges of the patches, attaching them to the backing at the same time—but you don't have to zigzag edges lying underneath other patches (Figure 22). Topstitching this way eliminates the bulk that would result if you turned under hems on the overlapping pieces. Trim the backing from the collage close to the stitching line. Zigzag the outer edges of the collage to your garment.

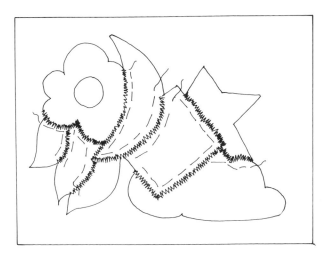

Fig. 22 Zigzag stitching edges of collage pieces to the backing fabric

TRIMS

Common trims are braid, ribbon, buttons, beads, and sequins. These can be used to hide mended or stained areas, as well as to outline designs and borders. They also add detail and texture to patches and appliques. If you buy new trims, though, they may be too bright to go well with the subtle colors of old clothes. You can get an "antique" look by staining trims made of natural fibers, for instance, cotton, linen or silk, in a solution of strong tea.

Or use old trims. Secondhand stores and thrift shops often have boxes of old lace trimmings and jars of old buttons. And damaged clothes may yield unusual beading or embroidery, or pieces of fabric that you can make into bias bands, patch pockets, detachable peplums, or use to cover sections like yokes and bib fronts.

Braids, ribbons, lace edgings, and other bands can be sewn under edges or topstitched to a garment. They can be sewn on by hand with a hemming or whipping stitch, or by machine with a straight or zigzag stitch. Machine sewing is faster and stronger. If the trim is narrow, one row of stitching down the center will hold it in place sufficiently. If it's wider, stitch it down on both edges. If the trim is being worked around a corner, miter it to make a neat point by folding the trim back on itself and stitching on the diagonal as shown in Figure 23. Then trim off the triangular excess. Fold the trim down the other side of the curve and continue stitching.

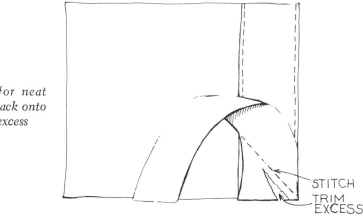

Fig. 23 To miter for neat corners, stitch trim back onto itself and cut off excess

STITCH
TRIM
EXCESS

Beads and sequins work best on jeans, satin blouses, dressy sweaters, and evening clothes. Lots of beads—buttons, too—will add weight and pull on the fabric, so use them only on sturdy garments. Sequins are extremely delicate and can be easily damaged when the garment is cleaned.

Sew beads and sequins on with a strong double thread. You can run the thread through beeswax to prevent twisting and breaking. Use a very fine needle. Special ones are made that are much longer and more flexible than normal needles and make your work much easier. If you're making a pattern with beads or sequins, trace the design on the fabric with tailor's chalk first.

Use thread that matches the fabric when sewing on beads. To sew beads on separately, bring the thread up from the underside of the fabric and through the bead. Then reinsert the needle, a bead's length away from where it first came through as shown in Figure 24. Rows of beads can be sewn on in two ways: individually with a backstitch as just described; or by stringing a row of beads on strong thread, then whip stitching the thread between each bead to the garment, as shown in Figure 25.

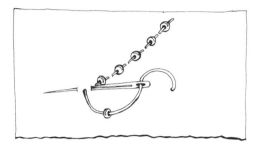
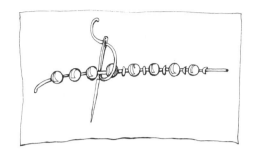

Fig. 24 *Beads sewn onto fabric individually with backstitch*

Fig. 25 *Beads are strung onto thread, then whip stitched onto fabric between each bead*

For sewing sequins, the thread should be the same color as the sequins. To sew them singly, place a small bead on top of each to hold it in place. Then bring the thread up through each sequin and bead and back down through the sequin again, as shown in Figure 26. To sew sequins on in rows, bring the needle up through the center of the sequin and take a backstitch. Pull the thread through until the sequin is flat against the fabric. Continue, overlapping the sequins as shown in Figure 27.

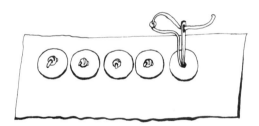
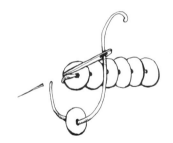

Fig. 26 *A tiny bead is used when sewing sequin into place*

Fig. 27 *Overlapping sequins as they're stitched on in rows*

EMBROIDERY

Embroidery is another way to decorate, as well as to camouflage mended and stained areas. It consists of various hand or machine stitches either done singly or combined to make patterns.

If you want to use a machine, make running, basting, or zigzag stitches in various lengths and different colored threads for patterns (Figure 28). Some of the newer sewing machines have special attachments for producing embroidery patterns. Or you can try the free-motion method which involves removing the presser foot from the machine, making the feed dog inoperative, and putting the fabric in an embroidery hoop:

maneuver it by hand to produce the patterns. Designs can be drawn on the fabric beforehand or you can make them free style—but this technique is rather difficult to do well and takes practice.

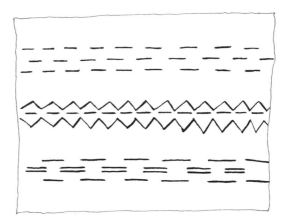

Fig. 28 Machine embroidery stitches

Hand embroidery is easier and allows you to use a greater variety of stitches. It's also relaxing and more satisfying aesthetically. Here are some supplies needed for hand embroidery.

Materials

THREAD

You can use thread that either blends or contrasts with the color of your garment, depending on the effect you want. The same color thread will give a subtle look, so use a variety of stitches to add interest and give texture. Contrasting thread colors will make the embroidery more obvious, so the stitches should be done as evenly and skillfully as possible.

There are several types of thread that can be used for embroidery: six-stranded silk, cotton, or rayon embroidery floss; single-stranded perle cotton; heavier, nontarnishing metallic thread; crewel or needlepoint yarn made of wool. Gear the type and thickness of the thread you use to your fabric. For example, use two strands of silk floss on chiffons and other lightweights; use three strands of cotton floss on medium weights; and use wool yarns on heavier, thicker fabrics.

NEEDLES

There are also different needle sizes that can be used for embroidery. Most common are the regular embroidery or crewel needles and the larger tapestry ones with blunt points and extra-large eyes. Again, the size of the needle you use will depend on the fabric you're working on. Don't use a needle that's too large or it will leave holes.

EMBROIDERY HOOPS

You may want to use an embroidery hoop to keep your work flat and even, though some stitches are easier to do without one. Wood hoops are good because the fabric doesn't slip as much as in a metal hoop. The size of the hoop should be near the size of the area you're working on—8 inches is standard. Arrange the fabric inside the hoop so the threads are on the straight of grain. And don't leave the hoop on the fabric an unnecessarily long time; it will leave a mark on the material.

Designs

If repairs or stains on your garment are small and few, you can do your embroidery free style, making the design as you go. Easy designs to make are florals, hearts, and butterflies. Use whatever strikes your fancy so long as the size and shape of the design is in proportion to your garment.

Fig. 29 Repeated embroidery patterns

If there is only one spot to be embroidered, repeat the design elsewhere on the garment so it won't look off balance (Figure 29). If there are several small areas to be embroidered, connect them with stitches so they won't look spotty (Figure 30).

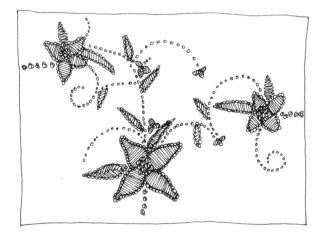

Fig. 30 Connecting designs with embroidery stitches

If you need to cover a larger area with embroidery, draw the design on the fabric first with a chalk pencil. If you don't feel sure drawing freehand, trace a design on tissue paper, making sure it fits adequately over the area you want to cover. Pin or baste the tissue paper to the garment, placing dressmaker's carbon paper in between. Transfer the

38

design with a pencil or other pointed object, so long as it's not sharp enough to poke through the paper. Work from top to bottom to avoid getting any carbon smudges on your garment (Figure 31). If you don't want to trace the pattern on, you can attach the tissue paper design to the fabric and work the embroidery stitches over the paper. Then tear the paper off when you are done.

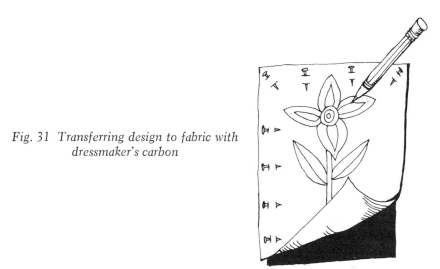

Fig. 31 Transferring design to fabric with dressmaker's carbon

If you aren't good at creating your own designs, you can buy ready-made patterns that are transferred to your garment by ironing. Lay the pattern on your garment ink side down, making sure its position is correct because the ink may not come off once it's ironed on. Press the design on by lifting the iron up and down over the pattern. Don't slide the iron heavily back and forth over the pattern or the ink may streak.

Stitches

There are many embroidery stitches, ranging from simple to intricate. When making them don't use overly long thread or it will get tangled. Knot or take small backstitches at the beginning and end of your stitching; keep stitches even—not too loose and not too tight.

Some common sewing stitches can be used for embroidery, such as the running stitch, backstitch, and buttonhole stitch. Here are descriptions of some of the simpler embroidery stitches.

Chain Stitch. A linked stitch that can be used singly or in numbers as a fill-in. To make it, bring the needle through from the underside and make a loop with the thread. Reinsert the needle where it first came through, then bring it up through the fabric and over the loop (Figure 32). Pull the threads gently to tighten the loop.

Lazy Daisy Stitch. One of many variations of the chain stitch used for floral patterns. To make it, bring the needle up, loop the thread and hold it in place. Insert the needle where it first came through, then bring it up at the loop. Take a small stitch over the loop to hold it down (Figure 33).

Satin Stitch. A smooth, even flat stitch. Make long, parallel stitches so close together that no background shows (Figure 34). You can give this stitch a padded look by working it over running stitches.

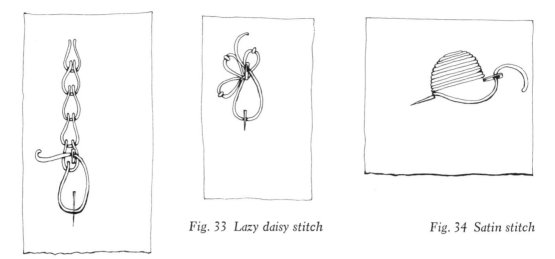

Fig. 33 *Lazy daisy stitch*

Fig. 34 *Satin stitch*

Fig. 32 *Chain stitch*

Cross Stitch. Another flat stitch made in the shape of Xs. Work a row of slanting stitches going one way (Figure 35). Then go back and complete the crosses by making another slanting row of stitches in the opposite direction, crossing exact centers of the first stitches. Keep the work even.

Fly Stitch. A looped stitch that can be worked vertically or horizontally. Make a loose horizontal stitch and bring the needle up at the center of the thread loop. Then take a small stitch that loops over the thread and pulls the stitch down as shown in Figure 36.

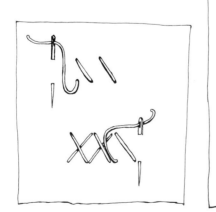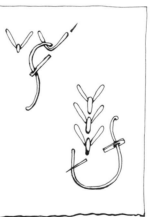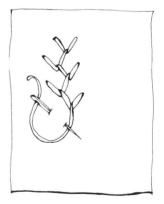

40   Fig. 35 *Cross stitch*   Fig. 36 *Fly stitch*   Fig. 37 *Feather stitch*

Decorating

Feather Stitch. A looped stitch that can be made in a straight line or doubled by taking two stitches to the left and then two to the right. For a straight feather stitch, make a loose horizontal stitch and bring the needle up at the center of it. Then take another stitch to one side of the first as shown in Figure 37. Continue alternating sides, looping the thread under the needle each time.

When you've finished stitching, press the embroidery from the wrong side. Use steam; place a towel between the iron and the fabric to keep the raised texture of the work.

DYEING

Dyeing can help bring new life to old clothes. Dark dye colors like brown, navy, and black will hide faded and worn spots and can cover some stains and yellowing. Dyeing can also tame harsh colors and tone down unattractive prints. Light-colored sheer fabrics can have their transparency camouflaged by being dyed a darker shade.

General Considerations
FABRICS

The fabric of your garment will determine how the dye color will take. The natural fibers of cotton, linen, silk, wool, and viscose rayon will give strong, long-lasting color. Synthetic fabrics, however, react unpredictably—some will take dye only slightly, giving a pastel shade; others won't take dye at all. Some old clothes are a combination of both natural and synthetic fibers. For example, you can find lingerie made from a synthetic fabric with lace trim made of cotton or silk. In this case the garment will often dye a soft pastel shade, whereas the lace will dye much darker.

Clean and mend your garment before dyeing it. When mending it's important to use the same type of thread as fabric—that is, either a natural or synthetic one. This way, when the garment is dyed, the thread will take the color the same way the fabric does.

DYES

Use all-purpose household dyes (Rit is a common one) for dyeing old clothes. These can be purchased at supermarkets. Or if you want even better results, you can use dyes sold at weaving shops. One good brand is Cushings, an inexpensive dye that gives strong color.

There are hot and cold-water dyes available. Hot-water dyes give strong color and have good staying power or fastness. The hot water, though, can shrink some fabrics; so be careful. Cold-water dyes give light rather than deep colors and aren't as resistant to fading as hot-water dyes.

Solid-Color Dyeing

Prepare the dye according to the package directions. Use soft water if possible because it will penetrate the fiber more easily than hard water. One-quarter teaspoonful 41 of Calgon water softener added to one pint of dye will help if you have hard water. Do the dyeing in a sink or bathtub or use unchipped enamel, glass, plastic, or stainless steel pans. Make sure your container is large so there is ample room for the garment and the water. If it's too small the dye may take unevenly. Wear rubber gloves and an apron to protect yourself.

If possible, experiment with the dye color on a scrap of fabric from the garment first. If your fabric is other than white or off-white, its existing color will work with the dye to produce a third color—for example, red over blue will make purple. So keep this in mind when planning your dye colors.

The garment should be wet before putting it in the dyebath. If it's not still wet from being washed, immerse it first in water. This helps the penetration of the dye and gives a stronger, more even color. Use a large wooden spoon to stir and to gently poke the garment down into the dyebath throughout the process to further ensure even color distribution. The color will seem quite dark, but remember that it will be lighter when the material is dry.

Rinse several times by immersing the fabric in water rather than holding it under the tap. Wrap the garment in a towel to absorb excess moisture. Then lay it out flat on another towel or on a large piece of plastic. *Don't hang the garment*: the dye can migrate if there's too much water left in. Press when the fabric is still slightly damp; heat helps to set the color.

If the color has not turned out dark enough or is streaked and uneven, redye it until you are happy with the results. Subsequent washings of your dyed garment should be done with care. Use cool water, a mild soap, and wash separately to maintain the color.

Tie Dyeing

Basically, tie dyeing involves either knotting, folding, and tying, or stitching fabric so that when it's submerged in dye only the untied areas are colored. The tied areas resist the dye, picking up just a small amount—thus making patterns which are revealed when the garment is untied. You can use one or several colors; you can have a tie-dyed effect in one area only or all over the fabric. The important thing is not the number of ties you make, but how the patterns and colors relate to each other and your garment.

This is usually done on light to medium weight fabrics that are white or pastel in color. You can also tie dye print fabric as long as the background color is light and it's made from a natural fiber. This way the tie dye pattern will be dark and will add interest and color to the original print.

The possibilities for tie dye patterns are endless. Your patterns will be determined by the method of tying, the spacing, and the number of colors you use. Whatever method of tying you employ, make sure it's done tightly enough so it will resist the dye. If your ties are too loose you will lose the pattern. Here are some basic ways to tie your fabric before dyeing it.

KNOTTING

Knotting is the simplest method of "tying" (Figure 38). Knots that are tightly made, though, are sometimes hard to undo. Try untying knots when the fabric is still in the rinse water or secure a nonmetal object, such as a stick or a piece of rope, in the knot when you first make it. Then just pull on the stick or untie the rope and the knot will come undone.

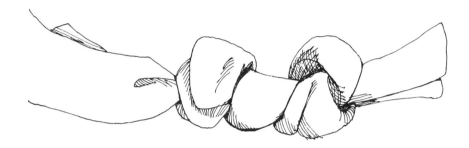

Fig. 38 Knotting fabric for tie dyeing

FOLDS

Folds and pleats can be made large or small to give various patterns. You might want to try them out on paper first to see what the design is like. After being folded the fabric is tied or clipped so it stays in place (Figure 39). To tie, use buttonhole or carpet thread, string, yarn, tape, fishing line, rubber bands, or fabric strips. These must be strong so they can withstand the pulling when you tighten them around the fabric. Also, only sturdy fabrics can be tied, so consider the condition of the fabric beforehand. The pattern will be determined by the type of fastening you use, its width, its tightness, and its placement on the fabric. A quick way to create folds is to bunch the fabric up and put it in a net bag or a piece of mesh, then tie tightly around it before dropping it into the dye.

Fig. 39 Folds and pleats are tied tightly

PROCEDURE

Before you put your "tied" garment into the dyebath, read the preceding section, *Solid-Color Dyeing.* If you want a soft-edged pattern effect, don't wet the garment before dyeing it. If you've never tie dyed before, it might be wise to practice first on old T-shirts or fabric scraps.

1. "Tie" the fabric.
2. Wet the material if you want a sharp-edged effect; leave dry for softer patterns.
3. Dye the fabric.
4. Rinse very well so there will be no bleeding when you untie.
5. Untie the fabric, dry till slightly damp, then press.

Variety can be added to your patterns by use of more than one color. This is done by dyeing over the first color with a second. For example, if your pattern color is blue, dyeing over it with yellow will give green. Follow these steps: untie the fabric after the first dyeing; retie it; then redye it another color. If you want several colors, follow this procedure between each dyebath.

4 /
RECYCLING

There's an abundance of rich, old fabrics, such as silk scarves, lace tablecloths, and chenille bedspreads, that can be easily changed into personal, stylish looking clothes. Some items can be made wearable by simply wrapping or tying them around your body in imaginative ways. Old piano covers are a good example: they're large squares, often silk, with elaborate embroidery and long fringe on the edges. A piano cover is a natural as an evening shawl or tied around your waist as a dramatic second layer over wide-legged pajamas or a long skirt. Or it can be worn alone—wrapped around your hips, sarong style. Watch for unusual fabrics in large or small pieces when cleaning out attic trunks, scavenging in junk stores, or while at swap meets. Bed linens, table linens—even furniture throws—may have real possibilities. You'll unearth patterns and prints that are truly outstanding—and quite rare; if fabric is in good enough condition to work with easily, you can create truly unique garments this way.

While this section is mainly about recycling items not originally meant to be worn, don't overlook the possibilities of cutting up old dresses or suits for fabrics. Often these pieces aren't large enough to make one complete garment, but you can seam them together, patchwork style. Or use commercial patterns with small construction pieces; for example, gores, tiers, yokes, or set-in sleeves.

SCARVES

Old scarves were generally made of silks or soft rayons, with unusual prints and muted colors. They can be worn as head scarves, handkerchief skirts, or as bare, wrapped tops like the ones shown here.

Wrapped Tops

Bare Triangle. Fold a square scarf in half on the diagonal to form a triangle. Knot in back, as shown in Figure 40.

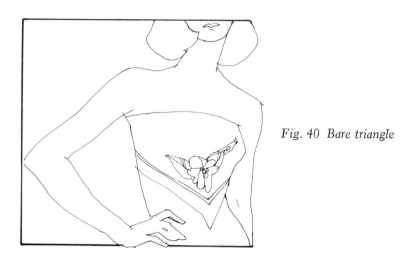

Fig. 40 Bare triangle

Bandeau. Fold a square scarf into a triangle, then fold the point of the triangle up as shown in Figure 41a. Knot the scarf in front or back (Figure 41b).

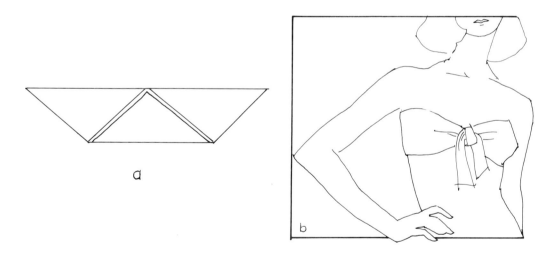

Fig. 41 a, Scarf is folded into a triangle, then folded again; b, bandeau

Bandeau Twist. Fold a large square scarf as shown in Figure 41a. Twist the scarf in front and tie the ends behind your neck as shown in Figure 42.

46

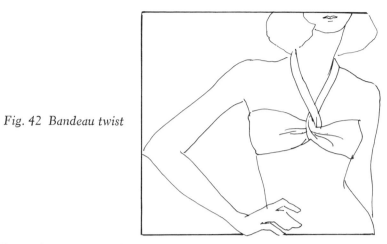

Fig. 42 Bandeau twist

Crisscross Top. Wrap a long rectangular scarf, no less than 10 inches wide, around your neck. Cross it in back or in front and tie as shown in Figure 43.

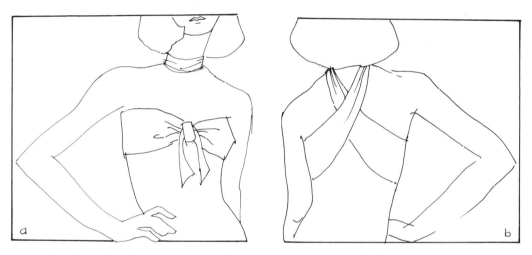

Fig. 43 a, Scarf is wrapped around the neck; b, then crossed in back for crisscross top

Ribbon Halter. Fold a square scarf into a triangle. Turn the point under a few inches and stitch it down to make a casing for a ribbon. Then trim the point off close to the stitching line. Insert ribbon in the casing, then tie the ribbon behind your neck and knot the points of the scarf behind your back (Figure 44).

Fig. 44 Ribbon halter

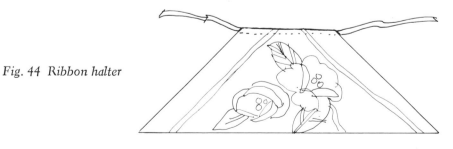

Handkerchief Skirt

Large scarves convert naturally into the handkerchief-hemmed skirt pictured in Figure 45. If you can't find scarves large enough to make the skirt as long as you'd like, just sew on a second tier of scarves.

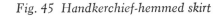

Fig. 45 Handkerchief-hemmed skirt

1. Find four large, square scarves of the same size in patterns and colors that blend.

2. Sew the scarves together to form one large square; press the seams open as shown in Figure 46a.

3. Fold the large square back down to the size of one scarf. Then measure your hips (say 36 inches) and divide the amount by four (9 inches). Cut a quarter circle, the circumference of which is 9 inches, out of the center of the folded square as shown in Figure 46b.

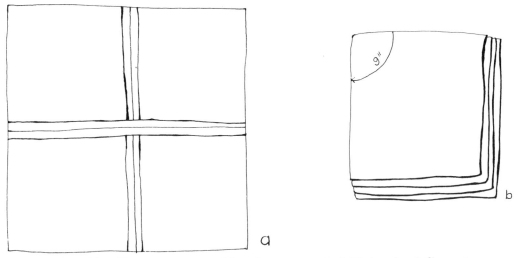

Fig. 46 a, Four scarves seamed into large square; b, folded and waistline cut

4. To make an elasticized waist, first open the square out. Then make a self-casing and insert an elastic band on the circle edge, following steps 3 and 5 under *Petticoat,* Chapter 6.

DRAPERY

Old drapery fabrics often have large floral prints. To take advantage of these designs, use patterns that have large construction pieces. A wraparound skirt is a perfect candidate because it can be made without seams, allowing a large, splashy pattern to show in full. The valance or top pleated portion of the drape can also be used; for instance, inverted at the waist of a midriff top. Here's how J.J. made such a top, as well as a matching wrapped skirt (Figure 47).

Fig. 47 Drapery into midriff top and wraparound skirt

49

Midriff Top

Cut the valance from the drape so it fits from under your arms to just above your waist. The pleats of the valance should fit snugly around your midriff. Cut ½ inch extra on all edges for seam and hem allowances. Make a casing on the top edge and insert an elastic band as in steps 3 and 4, under *Petticoat*, Chapter 6. Baste the edges together at the center back and insert a zipper (see Chapter 2, under *Worn Closures*). Make straps out of wide ribbon or excess drapery fabric. If you use fabric, follow the directions for making ties in step 15, under *Wrap Dress into Peplum Top*, Chapter 5. Attach the straps with a hand stitch.

Wraparound Skirt

Use a commercial pattern to make a wrapped skirt or simply wrap the drapery fabric around your waist 1½ times. Then cut the side edges of the skirt at slight A-shaped slants and finish all the edges with a narrow machine-stitched hem. Make long ties out of excess drapery fabric, following step 15 under *Wrap Dress into Peplum Top*, Chapter 5. Attach them to the waist edges with a hand stitch.

LACE TABLECLOTHS

Shawls, Ponchos, and Capes

Old lace tablecloths can be made into delicate, romantic clothing. A simple transformation is to make a shawl by folding or cutting the tablecloth in half on the diagonal.

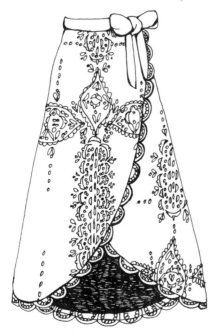

Fig. 48 Lace tablecloth into wrap skirt with ruffled edge and satin tier

Fig. 49 Ruffle extends only partway up underneath edge

Then edge it with silk fringe or eyelet ruffles. You can make a poncho from a round tablecloth by cutting a circle in the center for your head and finishing the edge with a narrow hand-stitched hem. Or use a commercial pattern and a large tablecloth to make an elegant, hooded, floor-length cape for evening wear.

Lace tablecloths also make fragile-looking skirts and tops. Use any pattern you like, keeping the lace see-through if you feel provocative, or backing it with lightweight fabric, perhaps in different colors.

Ruffle-Edged Wrap Skirt

Mary McCray made the wrapped skirt illustrated in Figure 48. She rounded the edges and trimmed them with a lace ruffle for variation.

Follow the instructions for a basic wraparound skirt in the preceding section, under *Drapery*. To prevent bulkiness when you wrap the skirt, extend the ruffle only partway up the underneath edge as shown in Figure 49. Then finish the remainder of the edge with a narrow hem. Attach doubled satin ribbon to the top edge for waistband and ties.

CHENILLE BEDSPREADS

Soft, warm bedspread fabrics like chenille make cuddly full-length robes. Because of the bulky nap of chenille, it's easier to make a garment that doesn't have much detailing or gathering. Use heavy duty thread and needle and, if you're using a machine,

Fig. 50 Chenille bedspread into caftan

51

watch the nap carefully because it has a tendency to catch in the hole at the needle. Also, be sure when you're laying out your pattern pieces that the nap is going in the same direction on each piece. Wash and dry chenille fabric, but don't press it. Instead, shake it out and brush the nap with a fairly stiff brush to restore its fluffiness.

Caftan

Here's how to make a simple caftan from a chenille bedspread (Figure 50).

1. Use a commercial pattern for your caftan or use a slipover lounging garment you already have, similar to the one illustrated, as a pattern.

2. Fold the bedspread in half and pin your pattern or old caftan on the fabric as shown in Figure 51.

3. Cut out the caftan. If you're using a garment for your pattern, be sure you make the neck large enough so it will slip over your head easily, since it will be the only opening. And leave ½ inch extra on the side and underarm edges for seam allowances.

4. Stitch the underarm and side seams. Instead of hemming, finish the neck, sleeve, and bottom edges with fold-over braid, being sure to catch both edges of the tape as

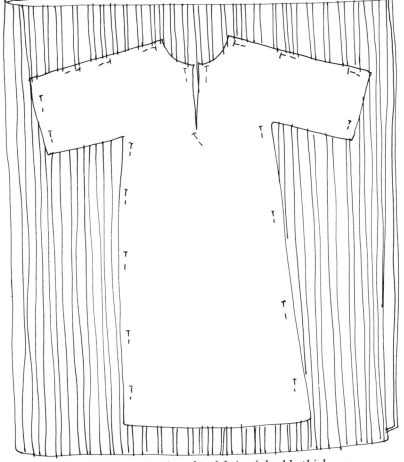

Fig. 51 Pattern is pinned to fabric of double thickness

you stitch. You can add fringe to the sleeves if you like, though it tends to get in the way when you're doing things like cooking and washing dishes. You could also make a sash belt out of excess fabric, following step 15 under *Wrap Dress into Peplum Top*, Chapter 5.

Fig. 52 Wrapped robe, combining parts from commercial and handmade patterns

Wrapped Robe

Figure 52 shows a more complicated robe that can be made from chenille: it is an example of the kind of thing that can be done if you're adept at pattern drafting.

J.J. and Laurie put it together by combining new and old, commercial and home-made patterns. The wrapped skirt and bodice were cut from a modern robe pattern. The shawl collar was made by making a paper pattern from a favorite shawl-collared sweater.

The sleeve was tricky because there was no pattern for it, just a picture in an old pattern book. (The one used was *Modern Pattern Design* by Harriet Pipin, Funk and Wagnalls, 1942.) A sleeve pattern was drafted from the picture by using a basic sleeve pattern like the one shown (Figure 53*a*), then adding onto, cutting, and slashing into it so it was like the one in the book (Figure 53*b*). The hem was finished with seam binding.

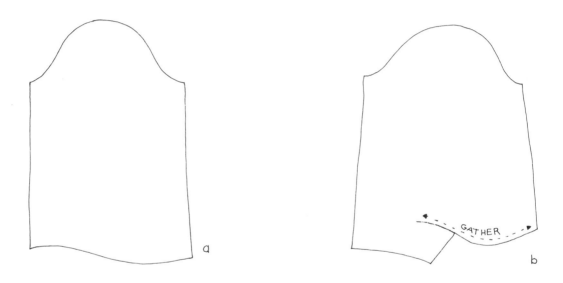

Fig. 53 a, *Basic sleeve pattern;* b, *pattern reworked to achieve authentic style*

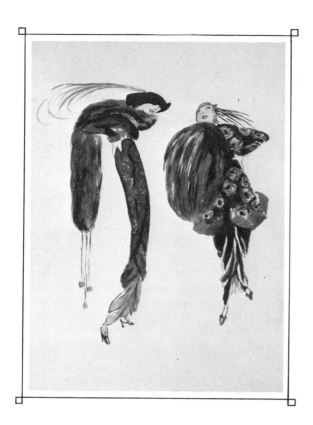

5 /

REMODELING DRESSES

She had gowns of velvet like poured country cream . . . and chiffon that spiralled about her like golden smoke.
— Dorothy Parker

Old period dresses come in a rich assortment of fabrics and styles that is hard to duplicate today. You can find rare fabrics like silk (butter) velvet and one-of-a-kind deco prints. There's also a variety of styles available from the ornate, Slavic/Oriental look of the 1910s to the simple jersey suits of the 1930s.

Generally, more time and attention went into the construction of old dresses than into those manufactured today. They often have hand-finished hems, closures, and decorative features such as embroidery.

Because these dresses are old, they're obviously not going to be in top-notch condition—seams may need reinforcement, buttons or belts may be missing. You can add a variety of accessories to replace missing elements or to liven up these old clothes. Use antique or hand-painted buttons, lace trims, silk scarves, or beads. Here's where a little imagination can save you a lot of money and create a totally personal look.

While each dress presents a new problem, there are some typical areas that often need adjustment. In this section there are some suggestions for changing hems or necklines; for taking in sleeves, shoulders, and waistlines. There's also an example of taking in an entire bodice that's too big. Before you start a remodeling project, check through the tips in *Remodeling Guide.*

REMODELING GUIDE

Whether you're making simple alterations or starting a major remodeling job, there are some tried-and-true guidelines applicable to all such projects in this chapter. If you follow these recommendations, you'll be much happier with the results of your labors.

Before Beginning. Read all the instructions for a particular remodeling change first.

Trying On. Try the garment on throughout the remodeling process to make sure of the fit, especially when you're pinning new seams.

Seam Allowance. Use ½ inch seam allowance when cutting fabric or sewing.

Pressing. Press seam allowances open after sewing the seam. Press the garment completely when finished.

Backstitch. Backstitch (reverse stitch) or fasten the threads at the beginning and end of all stitching.

HEMS

Different hem lengths abound on old dresses and fortunately for us varying lengths are in style today. You'll look good in anything from Victorian floor-length petticoats to knee-hitting flapper dresses. There will be times, however, when you'll want to alter the hem on period dresses to make them look just right for you. Here are a few suggestions.

Shortening

It's easier to shorten than lengthen a hem because it's mainly a matter of cutting off the excess. This can be done at the top or bottom edge of the skirt. (For instructions on shortening at the waistline, see steps 1–5, under *Petticoat*, Chapter 6.) Before hemming, try the garment on with the shoes you plan to wear. Then decide how much excess to cut off, and measure accurately all the way around so the hem will be even. If you're doing the measuring yourself, stand in front of a full-length mirror and check the hem from every angle to be sure it hangs properly. The traditional and more accurate way, though, is to use a skirt marker which measures the hem from the floor up. The best way to use the marker is to have a friend do the marking for you while you stand still.

After you've cut off the excess, finish the hem in a manner appropriate to the fabric. A good rule, if you're not sure, is to duplicate the original hem finish. The most common hem finish for light and medium-weight fabrics is to press or stitch the raw edge under ¼ inch. Then turn the edge up to the desired hem depth and either hand or machine

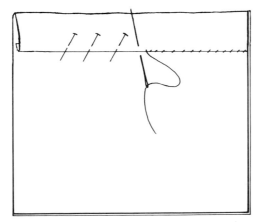

Fig. 54 Invisible hemming stitch

Fig. 55 *Chiffon is hemmed with zigzag stitch; excess fabric becomes a scarf*

57

Fig. 56 Circular ruffle of complementary fabric lengthens narrow skirt

stitch it to the dress. Machine stitching is the fastest way and makes a sturdy hem: use it for casual clothes, since the stitching will show on the right side. Or, for an invisible hem, do the final stitching by hand using a hemming stitch, as shown in Figure 54.

With fabrics that are bulky or that tend to ravel, finish the raw edge with seam or hem tape. Stitch the tape ¼ inch from the raw edge, then turn the edge up the desired amount and hem.

Some lightweight fabrics don't need a turned-up hem. Instead, you can simply finish the bottom edge with a zigzag stitch, as was done on the chiffon dress illustrated in Figure 55. If the fabric is very slippery, first roll the edge and then zigzag over it. Because the fabric is so soft and light, you could use the cut-off piece as a sash, neck scarf, or turban.

Lengthening with Ruffles

If you want to lengthen an old dress, one way would be to add a circular ruffle. A circular ruffle is not gathered at the top and so blends well with the styles of period clothes; it doesn't create the peasant look often associated with a gathered ruffle. To make it, find fabric comparable in weight to your garment and of a complementary or contrasting color or print. Whatever fabric you use, repeat it somewhere else—at the waist or neck, for instance—to balance the look.

If you have a relatively narrow skirt like the one illustrated in Figure 56, you can make a ruffle out of a single piece of old or new fabric.

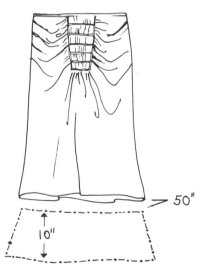

Fig. 57 Circumference of skirt is measured, length of ruffle determined

CONTINUOUS CIRCULAR RUFFLE

1. Undo the hem; if it is soiled along the fold line, cut it off. Then measure the circumference of the bottom edge of the dress (50 inches, for example). Decide the amount of length you want to add (say 9 inches) and add 1 inch for seam and hem allowances (10 inches total; Figure 57).

2. Make a pattern for the ruffle by marking off on paper a quarter circle which measures half the circumference of the hem (25 inches) plus an additional ½ inch for seam allowance and error.

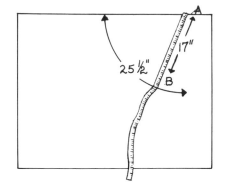 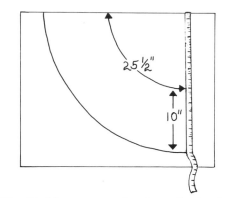

Fig. 58 *A quarter circle is marked off after determining length from point A to point B*

Fig. 59 *Measurement for the ruffle depth is added and another quarter circle completed*

To draw your quarter circle, pin or just hold the end of the tape measure at point A, as shown in Figure 58; mark off the form of a quarter circle as shown. To determine the length of the tape measure from point A to point B, take your circumference (51 inches) and divide by 3 (or 3.14 if you're mathematical) to get the 17-inch tape length. This will give you a quarter circle with a 25½-inch arc, which is half the circumference of the hem.

3. Add the ruffle length measurement (10 inches) to the outside of this curve and draw in another quarter circle, as shown in Figure 59.

4. Place one straight end of the pattern on the fold of the fabric, cut out the ruffle, and open it out. It is now a half-circle shape.

5. Seam the ends of the ruffle, closing the circle, and make a narrow hand or machine-stitched hem (Figure 60).

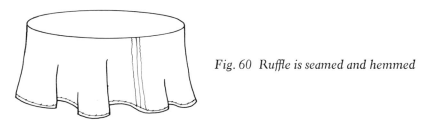

Fig. 60 *Ruffle is seamed and hemmed*

6. Clip the curve of the top edge. Seam the top of the ruffle to the bottom edge of the dress, matching the ruffle seam to the center back of the dress. Press the seam allowance up toward the dress.

SEPARATE RUFFLES

If you need a ruffle for a fuller skirt (say, 100 inches in circumference), you may need to make separate ruffles which are then sewn together. Doing it this way eliminates the problem of trying to find a single piece of fabric large enough to make this ruffle. Here's how to attach four fabric pieces to make one full ruffle for a 100-inch circumference skirt.

1. Undo the hem and, if it is soiled along the fold line, cut it off. Measure the circumference of the bottom edge of the skirt (100 inches). Decide the amount of length you want to add on (9 inches) and add 1 inch for seam and hem allowances (10 inches).

2. To make a pattern for the four small ruffles, draw a circle on paper whose circumference is one quarter the skirt circumference. For a 100-inch skirt, the small circle would be 25 inches around (Figure 61).

3. Add the length measurement (10 inches) around the edge of the circle and draw another circle outside the first as shown in Figure 61. Make a straight line on the pattern to mark where the straight of grain should be.

4. Cut out the pattern. Make a cut parallel to the straight of grain line, then cut out the inner circle.

5. Pin the circular pattern to one piece of fabric, matching the grain lines. Cut out the ruffle (Figure 62). The other three pieces are cut in the same manner.

6. Piece the individual ruffles by seaming them together at the sides into a complete circle. Machine or hand stitch a narrow hem on the bottom edge.

7. Clip the curve along the top edge of the ruffle and seam it to the bottom edge of the dress. Press the seam allowance up.

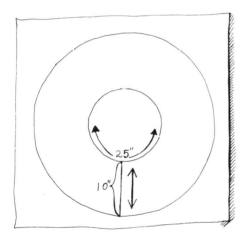

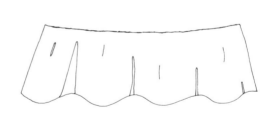

Fig. 61 *Inner circle is drawn, ruffle length added, outer circle drawn to complete pattern*   Fig. 62 *One-fourth of the ruffle at a time is cut from fabric*

NECKLINES

Necklines in period dresses are often a major style feature. Usually they have detailing, such as tiny tucks, cutout designs, or other decorative trims. In some dresses the whole bodice may be intricately draped from neckline to waistline. Because of these features it's hard to change just the neckline without disturbing the overall design of the

61

dress. But sometimes collars can just be cut off or a relatively plain or yoked neckline recut.

For example, high neckbands found on turn-of-the-century garments are often too tight, or are worn and frayed at the edges. You can cut off the neckband and replace it with another band of lace that fits and is in better condition. If the band you add looks too new for the garment, try staining it with a solution of strong tea for an antique look. Or you can form entirely new necklines; several examples follow.

Victorian High Neck into Square Neck

High-necked Victorian blouses and dresses were often pieced together with lace insets or yokes. This makes it easy to alter the neckline, as was done on the damaged high-neck bodice with a square yoke shown in Figure 63.

If you make a similar change, you will now have a neckline that is quite low and may be too full. Gather up any fullness, then add a border of wide eyelet or other lace trim. Seam, or overlap and topstitch, the trim to the dress. Miter the trim at the corners as shown in Figure 23.

Fig. 63 Damaged high-neck Victorian bodice transformed into square-necked version

Fig. 64 Rounded '30s neckline into low V neck

63

You can taper the new front neckline into the back neckline at the shoulder seams or you can reshape the back to match the front if you can work gracefully around the back buttons. If you do reshape the back, sew buttons or other fasteners to the added trim.

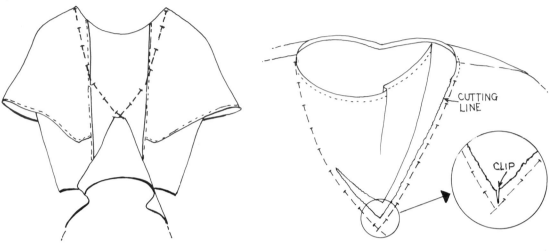

Fig. 65 *New neckline is tapered to meet the original back neckline at shoulders*

Fig. 66 *Cut outside the pin line, clipping V to turn smoothly*

Round Neck into Low V Neck

You can also lower high necklines on old dresses by cutting them into U or V shapes. The high, round neckline of the '30s chiffon dress in Figure 64 was changed into a V shape and tapered at the shoulders into the original back neckline. It was finished by turning under a narrow hem. It could also be finished by sewing tape or seam binding to the edge, then turning it to the inside and hemming it down.

1. Put the dress on right side out. Use pins to mark the outline of the new neckline. Taper the neckline at the shoulder seams so that it lines up evenly with the outer edge of the back neckline (Figure 65).

2. Cut ½ inch outside the pin line, starting from one shoulder seam, working toward the center, and back up to the other shoulder seam. Clip the center of the V, stopping just above the pin line (Figure 66). This will enable the point of the neckline to lie flat when it is hemmed.

3. Finish the neck edge with a narrow hem, rolling the raw edge under twice and attaching it with a slipstitch. Try to make a smooth transition between the hems of the new and old necklines where they meet at the shoulder seams. And take several extra stitches at the point of the V to reinforce it.

4. Put the dress on again, right side out. Since the neckline is now lower, there may be extra fullness around the bust which will need to be gathered. Pinch in the fullness where the gathers should be and mark each end of this area with pins (Figure 67).

5. To gather, make small running stitches on the right side of the dress between the two pins. Use a knotted thread and stitch ¼ inch from the hemmed edge. Take several stitches onto the needle first, then pull the needle through and gather the fullness

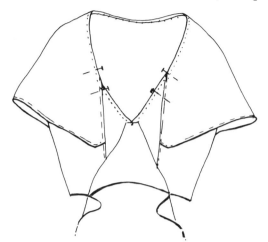

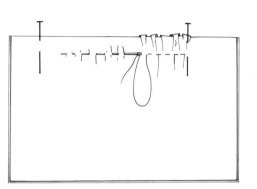

Fig. 67 Mark the areas where extra fullness needs to be gathered

Fig. 68 Take small stitches on right side and work gathers evenly

by pushing the fabric along the thread toward the knot, as shown in Figure 68. Continue until you've gathered all the fullness evenly, then knot the thread securely on the underside and remove the pins. To secure gathers, you can topstitch around the entire neckline, ¼ inch from the edge.

SLEEVES

If the sleeves on your dress are too large or are stretched out of shape, you can do several things—insert pads to lift the fullness at the sleeve cap; take tucks or pleats to

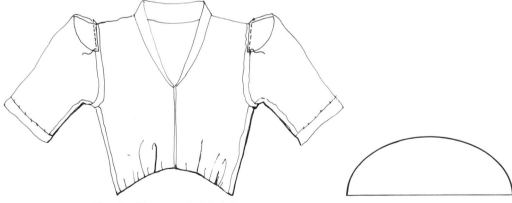

Fig. 69 Sleeve pads lift fullness

Fig. 70 Pattern shape for sleeve pad

bring in the fullness at the bottom sleeve edge; or elasticize a droopy sleeve so it's drawn up into a graceful, draped effect.

65

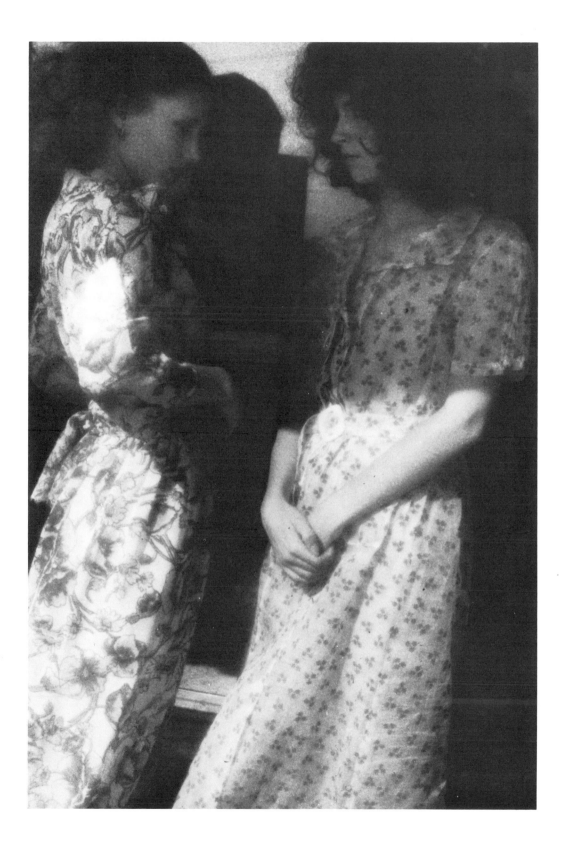

68

Sleeve Pads

A semicircular pad will lift a small amount of fullness and give a puffed look to the cap of the sleeve (Figure 69). This pad can be made from any stiff material, such as taffeta or various interfacings.

Measure the cap of the sleeve and cut a semicircular shape to size (Figure 70). Cover the stiff material with soft cotton so it's more comfortable next to your skin. Place the straight edge of the pad on top of, or just outside, the armhole seam stitching. Sew it in place with a hand running stitch or machine stitch, being careful not to sew into the sleeve.

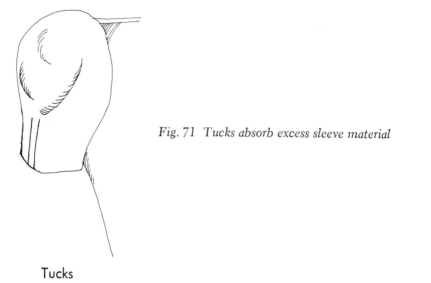

Fig. 71 Tucks absorb excess sleeve material

Tucks

One or two tucks taken on the bottom edge of the sleeve, as shown in Figure 71, will give a more fitted look. Take in excess by making one or two folds and pinning them

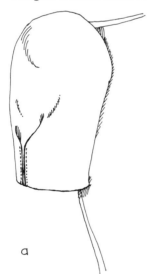

a

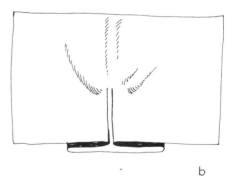

b

Fig. 72 a, Inverted pleats; b, folding sleeve pleats

down on the wrong side of the sleeve. Mark the length of the tucks with pins and then stitch them, following the directions for shoulder tucks in the next section of this chapter. Press the tucks flat.

Pleats

Another way to take in fullness is to make inverted pleats at the center bottom edge of the sleeve (Figure 72*a*). Fold the pleats as shown in Figure 72*b*. Topstitch each side of the pleat to hold it in place.

Elasticizing

To elasticize sleeves, taking up excess length and giving them shape as shown in Figure 73, first try the dress on wrong side out. Decide how much you want to raise the

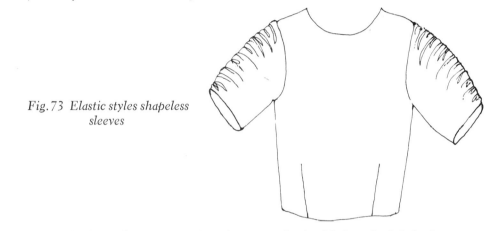

Fig. 73 *Elastic styles shapeless sleeves*

sleeve (say 4 inches), and cut two strips of narrow elastic this length. Mark the center bottom edge of each sleeve with a pin (Figure 74).

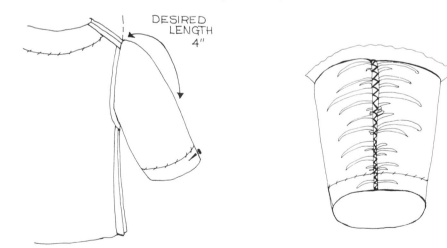

Fig. 74 *Measuring for finished sleeve length*   Fig. 75 *Wrong side of the elasticized sleeve*   71

Pin the elastic to the sleeve at the shoulder seam and the center bottom edge. Zigzag stitch it down, stretching the elastic as you go so it lies flat against the sleeve. When you are finished, the elastic will snap back bringing up the excess (Figure 75).

SHOULDERS

Wide shoulders are often a problem on old dresses. The solutions offered here range from simple shoulder pads to more decorative treatments—elasticizing, shirring, and tucks.

Shoulder Pads

One of the simplest ways to eliminate shoulder excess is to insert shoulder pads. Since they lift the fullness rather than take it in, as shirring does, for example, shoulder pads work best on moderately, not excessively, large shoulders. Here are two basic shoulder pad shapes: each lifts the fullness in a particular way.

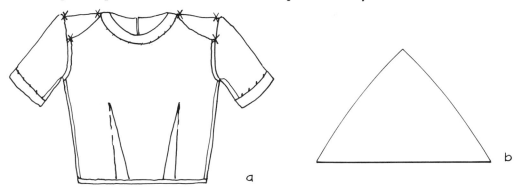

Fig. 76 a, *Traditional shoulder pads;* b, *the pattern shape*

TRIANGULAR

The traditional, triangular-shaped shoulder pad illustrated in Figure 76 will raise just the shoulder. You may be able to purchase this type shoulder pad in the notions section of your local department store. If not, you can easily make them yourself out of upholstery foam. Since the foam is available in various thicknesses, buy what you need, remembering that the thicker it is, the higher the lift. Cut the foam into a triangular shape the size of the shoulder area of your dress (Figure 76b). Cover the shoulder pads with soft fabric. Then tack them in place with four or five short stitches taken at the points marked with Xs. Tack them in lightly, since they should be taken out when you wash the garment.

EXTENDED

The triangular pad with a semicircular addition will *extend* the shoulder width as well as raise it (Figure 77). You probably won't be able to find it in a notions department, but it can easily be made out of foam. Follow the directions for making the pad

72

above but, instead of cutting the foam into a triangular shape, cut it into the shape shown in Figure 77b.

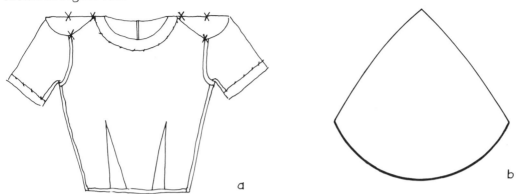

Fig. 77 a, *Extended pads lift both shoulders and sleeves;* b, *semicircular edge is added to triangular shape*

Elasticizing

Elasticizing is one of the simplest ways to take in shoulder fullness because all you do is stitch a piece of elastic to the shoulder seam. The elastic then pulls up the excess,

Fig. 78 *Elastic shoulder seams gather excess, create softly draping bodice*

creating folds that drape softly from the shoulder area (Figure 78). This technique works especially well on dresses made of soft, flowing fabrics.

1. Put the dress on and measure the desired shoulder length from neckline to sleeve. Cut a narrow strip of elastic this length for each shoulder (Figure 79*a*).

2. Take the dress off; on the wrong side, align the center of the elastic with the center of the shoulder seam. Pin the elastic to the shoulder at each end and in the middle (Figure 79*b*).

3. Sew the elastic to the shoulder seam with a zigzag stitch, keeping it stretched as you go. When you finish, the elastic will snap back, drawing up the excess.

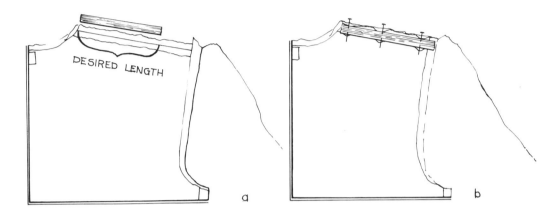

Fig. 79 a, *Measure length for finished seam;* b, *pin elastic at center and ends*

Tucks

Tucks are folds that take in excess fullness. The fullness is then released at one or both ends of the tucks, creating a draped effect. The number of tucks you take depends mainly on the design of the dress. In the dress illustrated in Figure 80, two shoulder tucks were taken because they complemented the two on each side of the peplum. The tucks were extended on either side of the shoulder seams so the excess would be taken in equally, front and back. The tucks could even be extended to the waistline if more bodice fullness needed to be taken in.

1. Try the dress on wrong side out. Measure the amount of fullness to be taken in on each shoulder. Divide this amount in two to get the width of each tuck. Then decide the length and placement of the tucks and mark with pins. The tuck length should be equal on both sides of the shoulder seam.

2. Make folds (tucks) in the fabric the desired width and length; pin them as shown in Figure 81. Tucks usually run parallel to the lengthwise threads of the fabric, along the straight of grain.

3. Sew on the pin line. Press the folds toward the center. You can also topstitch them in place for a decorative effect. Do not press directly below the stitch line, as that would flatten the release fullness.

74

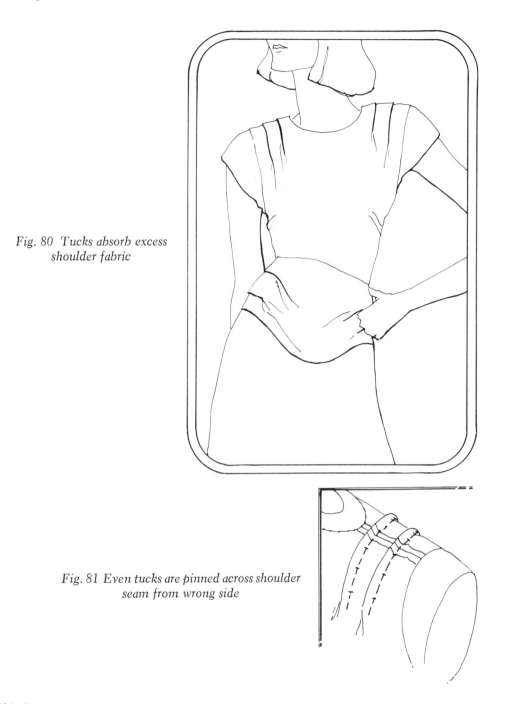

Fig. 80 *Tucks absorb excess shoulder fabric*

Fig. 81 *Even tucks are pinned across shoulder seam from wrong side*

Shirring

Shirring is actually several rows of gathering and is a decorative way to take up shoulder fullness on soft, lightweight fabrics. The gathering can be done with a special gathering foot that you attach to your sewing machine. It distributes the fullness evenly and then locks it in place as you sew.

75

Or, you can use elastic thread in the bobbin of your machine to make the gathers. If you do this, wind the elastic thread onto the bobbin by hand, stretching it only slightly. Then adjust the length of the stitch and the tension of your machine to get the desired fullness in the gathers.

If you don't have a gathering foot attachment or haven't sewn with elastic thread before, you might find it easier to follow the steps below. Double rows of gathers were used with spacing between them to create a design (Figure 82). Usually shirring rows are placed directly under one another, but use your imagination when deciding the placement and number of rows. Also, when you use shirring at the front of the shoulder as was done here, you will have to take in the corresponding back shoulder fullness.

Fig. 82 Shirring: double rows of gathers with space between create design

1. Put the dress on right side out. Determine what length the shoulder should be from neckline to sleeve. Mark the placement of the rows of shirring with pins. Undo the shoulder seam part way.

2. Machine baste for the double rows used here, starting from the sleeve edge and working to the neck edge. Pivot the fabric at the neck edge, take one stitch, then pivot again and sew back to the sleeve edge as shown in Figure 83.

3. When all the rows have been completed in this manner, pull up the threads and gather the shoulder fullness, distributing it evenly until the area measures the desired length. Then wind the threads around pins to secure the stitching (Figure 84).

4. Pull the threads through to the wrong side and tie them together. Stitch over the loose ends of the threads, securing them to the seam allowance (Figure 85).

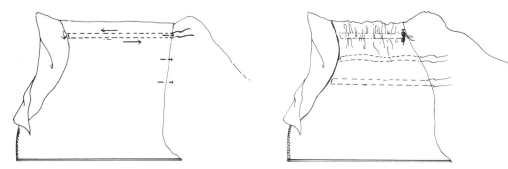

Fig. 83 Machine basting double rows   *Fig. 84 Distribute gathers evenly and secure threads*

5. Now take in the back shoulder fullness with tucks so it matches the length of the front shoulder at the seam. Do this by taking folds the needed amount and pinning them down. Resew the shoulder seam, locking the tucks in place (Figure 86).

6. Press the shoulder area, being careful not to place the iron directly on top of the shirring as this will flatten the gathers and spoil the effect. Instead, work the point of the iron into the area of fullness just below the shirring.

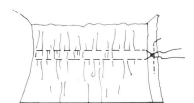
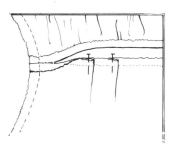

Fig. 85 Threads are pulled to wrong side and stitched down on seam allowance   *Fig. 86 Tucks in the back take up corresponding amount of fabric*

WAISTLINES

Large waists are a common problem with old dresses. Here are some suggestions on taking them in with belts, tucks, or darts.

Belting

Belting is the simplest way to take in waist fullness and create a dramatic change in style as well. For instance, the '20s chemise dress in Figure 87 seems wide and boxy by our standards. To update it, tie it at the waist with a long sash of satin ribbon or old

77

Fig. 87 Boxy long dress is transformed into blouson with simple addition of a belt

drapery cording. Then pull the dress up and slightly over the belt to create a blouson effect. This will shorten the length, take in the waist, and create a more flattering look.

Here's another easy belting technique. It works especially well on the long, full, lounging dresses of the '30s. Make a long tie out of ribbon or use excess fabric from the hem of the dress, following the instructions in step 15, under *Wrap Dress into Peplum Top*. Put the tie through the belt loops but, instead of tying it in front as you normally would, pull it to the back making a bow or knot. This pulls the fullness to the back and gives a sleek look to the front (Figure 88).

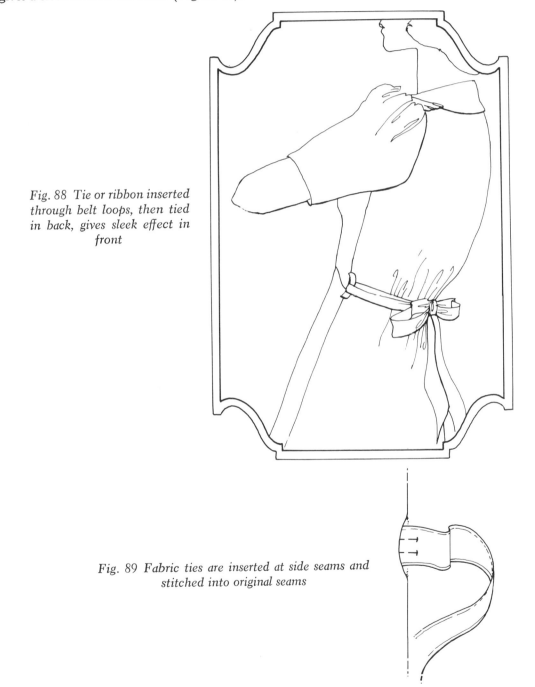

Fig. 88 Tie or ribbon inserted through belt loops, then tied in back, gives sleek effect in front

Fig. 89 Fabric ties are inserted at side seams and stitched into original seams

If the belt loops are missing from your dress or you want a different belting effect, insert two ties into the side seams as shown in Figure 89. Stitch along the original seam line. Then knot in the front or the back.

Tucks

Taking tucks at the waistline is another simple way to take in excess fullness. They can be sewn on top of, or into, the waistline seam; examples of both are given below. The number of tucks you use depends mainly on the style of the dress. Place them on both sides of the front or back at equal distances from the center.

The first example is a simple, full, wraparound '30s dress (Figure 90). Two front tucks were made on top of the waistline seam by dividing the excess equally into folds. The folds were then topstitched, placing the stitching directly over the stitching on the waistline seam.

Fig. 90 Tucks taken over the waistline seam to absorb excess fullness

In the second example, tucks were taken only in the bodice of the dress. They were inserted into the waistline seam so they wouldn't interfere with the look of the gored skirt (Figure 91). To make this kind of tuck, first undo the waistline seam across most

Fig. 91 Tucks take in fullness in bodice; excess skirt fullness is distributed along gore seams

of the center front. Then pin folds on both sides of the front to absorb the fullness. Take in the skirt a corresponding amount: do this by taking in a few of the seams of the front gored panels, distributing the excess equally between them. Or if the excess amount is enough, you can remove an entire gored panel. Resew the waistline seam, locking in the bodice tucks.

Darts

Darts are folds stitched on the wrong side of the garment and tapered to a point at one or both ends. Unlike tucks, which release the fullness, darts shape the excess to fit the curves of your body. But like tucks they are placed on either side of, and an equal distance from, the center front or back. Single-pointed darts can be made above and/or below the waistline seam of the dress. If, for example, you make darts on only the bodice, you will need to adjust the fullness of the skirt with tucks, darts, or gathers. Double-pointed darts can be easily made on dresses without a waistline seam. Here are examples of both.

81

SINGLE-POINTED DARTS

1. Try the dress on wrong side out and measure the amount of waistline fullness to be taken in (for example, 3 inches). Divide this amount in half to give you the width of each dart (1½ inches). With pins, mark the length and placement of the darts an equal distance above and below the waistline seam (Figure 92). Also make sure they are an equal distance from any existing darts.

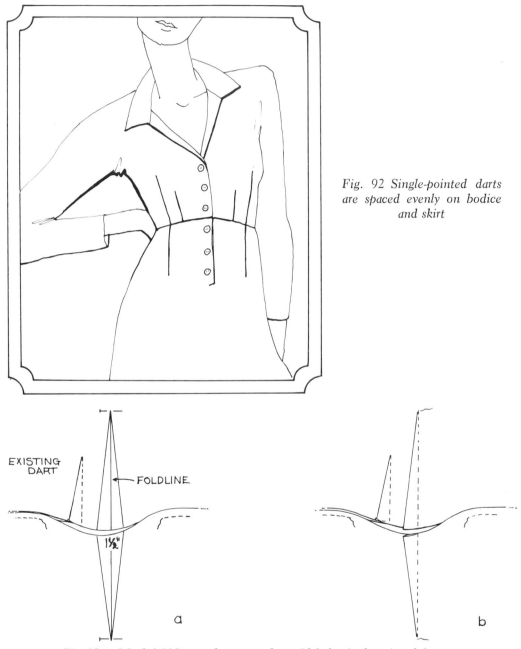

Fig. 92 Single-pointed darts are spaced evenly on bodice and skirt

Fig. 93 a, Mark fold line and measure dart width; b, single-pointed darts are incorporated into waistline seam

2. Take the dress off. Undo the waistline seam 2 to 3 inches on each side of the dart placement and make two corresponding darts on the bodice and the skirt. This will be less bulky than folding one long dart over the waistline seam.

3. Make the fold lines of the darts by drawing straight lines with tailor's chalk from the top and botton pins to the opened waistline seam. Then mark each dart width (1½ inches) at the waistline seam, centering the amount over the fold line. Draw chalk lines from the pins to the outer edges of the width as shown in Figure 93*a*.

4. Fold the darts in half along the fold lines and pin. Stitch them on the chalk line from the waistline to the point. Stitch directly onto the fold at the dart point to eliminate any puckering. Press the darts toward the center front (Figure 93*b*).

5. Resew the waistline seam.

Fig. 94 Double-pointed darts are used on garments without waistline seams

DOUBLE-POINTED DARTS

1. Try the dress on wrong side out and mark your waistline with tailor's chalk. Pinch in and measure the excess fullness at the waist (for example, 3 inches) and divide the amount in half to get the width of each dart (1½ inches). Decide on the placement of the darts—they should be an equal distance from the center front (Figure 94). Then   83

decide the length, marking the top and bottom with pins. Remember that these darts should be long, because they're giving shape to most of the torso.

2. Take the dress off. With tailor's chalk, draw a straight line connecting the top and bottom pins. This is the fold line of the dart. Then mark off the dart width (1½ inches) at the waistline, equally on both sides of the dart fold line. Draw chalk lines connecting the pins with the outer edges of the 1½ inch width as shown in Figure 95*a*.

3. Fold and pin the dart in half along the fold line. Stitch along the chalk line, beginning at the top point of the dart, working to the widest point at the waistline, and down to the bottom point. Stitch on the fold a little beyond both dart points to eliminate any puckering. Clip the fold line of the dart as shown so it will lie flat. Press the darts toward the center front (Figure 95*b*).

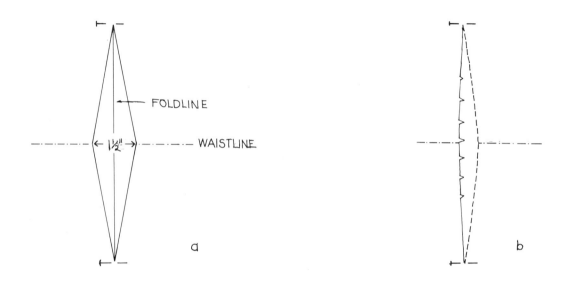

Fig. 95 a, Mark fold line and measure width of darts; b, clip darts along fold line and press toward center

BODICES

Old dresses are often too big throughout the entire bodice—including waist, bust, shoulders, and sleeves. Taking in all of these areas requires more time and experience than the previous remodeling suggestions. It involves removing and reinserting the sleeves and side zipper, and accurately recutting the armhole curve. It may also require readjusting the waistline or bustline darts, depending upon the amount taken in.

Even if you are an experienced seamstress, you may want to baste everything back into place before doing the final stitching. This way you can try the dress on to be sure of the fit. The effort is worth it, though, when the final result is a sleek-fitting dress like the one shown in Figure 96.

84

Fig. 96 Overly large, shapeless bodice can be transformed into a smooth style

85

1. Remove the sleeves from the dress by undoing the stitches at the armhole seams with a seam ripper. Set them aside for later.

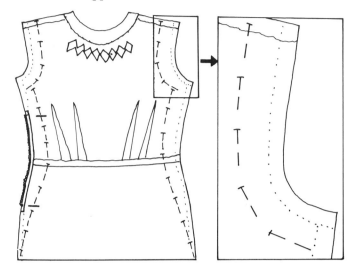

Fig. 97 Pin lines indicate new seams; closeup shows armhole, which must retain identical curve

2. Put the dress on wrong side out. Pinch in the side seams and pin them to fit, tapering below the waist to get a smooth line with the skirt. Because the side zipper will be cut off, mark the placement of the zipper stops with tailor's chalk on the pin line as shown (Figure 97). Mark with pins where the new armhole seams should be. Then take the dress off and check to be sure that the new armhole pin line maintains the original armhole curve. See the closeup of the curve in the box (Figure 97).

3. Take the dress off; on the wrong side, cut excess fabric from the armhole and side seams ½ inch outside the pin line (Figure 98).

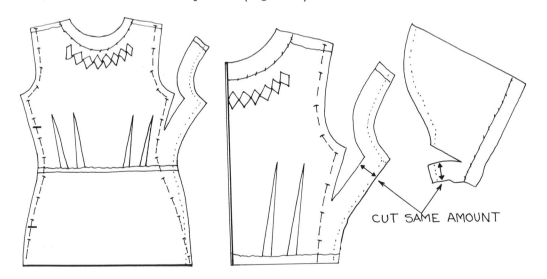

Fig. 98 Excess fabric is cut off, allowing ½ inch for seams

Fig. 99 Same amount of excess fabric is removed from side seam and underarm sleeve seam

4. Next, take in the sleeves you set aside earlier. To do this, note the amount of excess removed from the underarm side seam of the dress and cut this same amount from the sleeves as shown in Figure 99. Undo the hem a bit and seam the sleeve edges. Redo the hem.

5. Sew the side seams of the dress along the pin line. Remember to replace the belt loops at the waistline. When you come to one of the zipper-stop chalk lines, proceed as follows: backstitch to lock the seam, baste the length of the zipper opening, and backstitch again before continuing with the regular seam stitching (Figure 100). Press the seam allowance open.

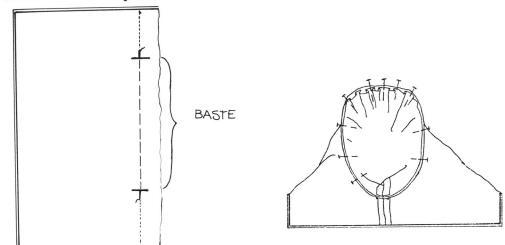

Fig. 100 *Zipper opening is basted when side seam is resewn*

Fig. 101 *Sleeve fullness is eased into the cap as sleeve is worked back into armhole*

6. Install the original zipper, following the instructions in steps 2–6 under Inserting a Zipper in Side of Dress, Chapter 2.

7. Still working on the wrong side, pin the sleeves into the new armholes, right sides together. Ease any fullness into the cap of the sleeve as you pin (Figure 101). Stitch the sleeves and clip the seam allowance at the underarm curves.

CONVERTING DRESSES INTO SEPARATES

A creative way to transform a baggy or unattractive dress is to make it into a skirt and top. You can cut the dress in half at the waistline and make a skirt out of the bottom part by adding a side zipper and a waistband. Or if the skirt is too large you can take in the side seams, elasticize it or insert a drawstring at the waist.

The top of the dress can be made into various blouses. If it is a shirtwaist style—that is, open down the front—and is large enough, you may be able to tie the shirttails together in front just above the waist. If the bodice is long enough, you can elasticize the bottom edge to create a blouson effect.

Here's how to change two dress styles—shirtwaist and wraparound—into peplum tops and skirts.

87

Fig. 102 *An ill-fitting shirtwaist is converted to nifty skirt and peplum top*

Shirtwaist into Skirt and Peplum Top

After cutting the dress in two, you can add contrasting or blending fabric at the waist to make a peplum on the shirtwaist top. Then use this fabric elsewhere as a neck scarf, hatband, or covered buttons to coordinate the look (Figure 102). A zipper was inserted in the skirt and grosgrain ribbon used for the waistband.

SKIRT

1. Remove the side zipper from the dress using a seam ripper. Detach the bodice from the skirt at the waistline seam.

2. Insert a zipper in the skirt using the lapped method, following the instructions on the zipper package.

3. Use 1½-inch-wide grosgrain ribbon to make a waistband. First measure the skirt waistline and add 2 inches for the waistband overlap. Buy twice this amount of ribbon, then double the layers to make a sturdier waistband. Turn the two raw ends of the ribbon under ½ inch each. Topstitch the ends together; continue stitching along one length of the ribbon, leaving the bottom edge open (Figure 103).

Fig. 103 Stitch along the length and ends of grosgrain ribbon, leaving one side open

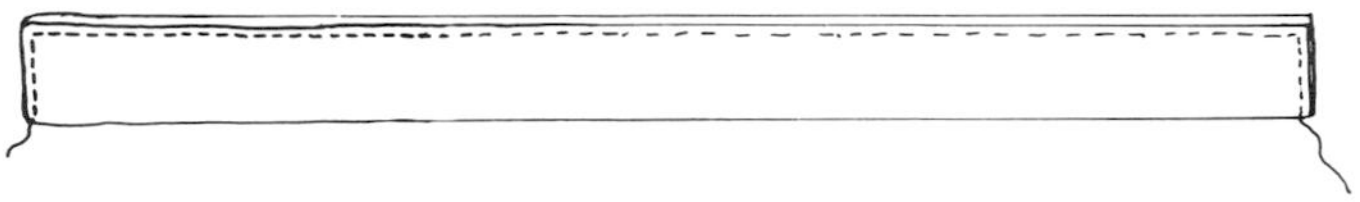

4. Sandwich the raw edge of the skirt waistline between the opened edges of the doubled ribbon. Then pin, leaving a 1½-inch overlap on the front part of the skirt at the zipper opening (Figure 104).

5. Topstitch all three thicknesses together as shown in Figure 105. Sew snaps on the ends of the waistband.

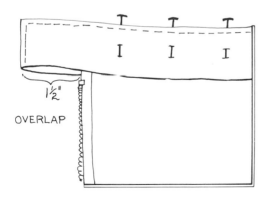

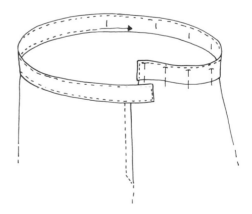

Fig. 104 Sandwich raw edge between layers of ribbon, leaving overlap at front zipper seam

Fig. 105 Topstitch through three layers

89

TOP

6. Try the bodice on to check the fit. The sides may now be too wide, since they were previously drawn in by the waistline seam. If they are, turn the top inside out and pin it to fit, tapering toward the underarm as shown (Figure 106). Sew along the pin line and cut off the excess.

Fig. 106 Pin in new side seams, tapering from waistline to armhole

7. Next make a paper pattern for the peplum. To do this, measure the circumference of the blouse waistline (say 26 inches) and decide what length you want the peplum to be (8 inches); Figure 107.

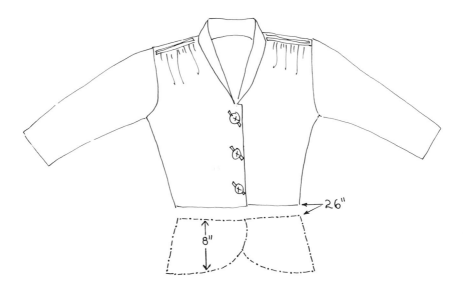

Fig. 107 Measuring for peplum pattern

8. Add 1 inch to the waistline measurement for the hem allowance. Then mark off this amount (27 inches) on a piece of string. Shape the string into a half circle, place

it on the paper, perhaps securing it with pins or tape, then draw this shape (Figure 108*a*).

9. Add the length measurement plus ½ inch (8½ inches) for a seam allowance to the outside of the half circle and draw another half circle as shown in Figure 108*b*. Curve the ends of the outer circle when cutting out the pattern.

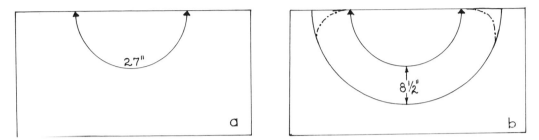

Fig. 108 a, Marking off half circle for pattern; b, length of peplum is added and another halfcircle completed

10. Cut the peplum out of a single thickness of fabric. Make a narrow hand or machine-stitched hem on the bottom edge of the peplum.

11. Turn the front bodice facings out. Line up the edge of the peplum hem with the facing fold (Figure 109) and pin. Then pin the rest of the peplum to the bodice, right sides together, and stitch.

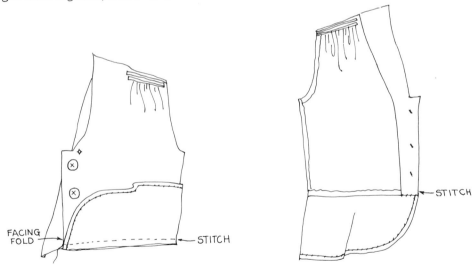

Fig. 109 Line up edge of peplum hem with front facing fold

Fig. 110 Facings are secured with a hand hemming stitch

12. Press the seam allowance toward the bodice and press the bottom edge of the facing up as well. Fold the facing back to its original position and attach it to the seam allowance with a hand hemming stitch as shown in Figure 110.

92   *Fig. 111 Oversized wrap dress transformed into peplum top and wraparound skirt*

Wrap Dress into Skirt and Peplum Top

This method involves cutting a too-large wrap dress in half below the waistline, creating a separate peplum top and wraparound skirt (Figure 111).

SKIRT

1. Try the dress on, right side out, and decide how far down you want the peplum to come. Remember, the longer you make the peplum, the shorter the skirt will be, so adjust accordingly.

Mark the peplum length with a pin. Remove the dress and measure the distance from the pin to the waistline seam. Continue measuring this distance and pinning all the way around.

2. Cut ½ inch outside of the pin line as shown (Figure 112).

Fig. 112 Measure length of peplum top and cut skirt off dress

3. Try the skirt on, wrapping the top edge around your waist 1½ times. If the skirt is larger than this (as this one was), place a pin where the top layer of the skirt should end.

4. Take the skirt off and continue pinning down the side of the skirt, following the slant of the other side as shown. Cut the excess off (Figure 113). Finish the raw edge with a narrow hand or machine-stitched hem.

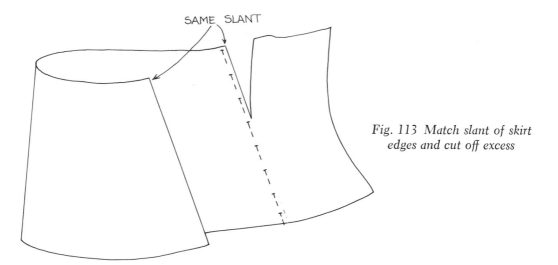

Fig. 113 Match slant of skirt edges and cut off excess

5. To make ties and a waistband, use ribbon or strips of fabric from the skirt excess as we did here. For 1½-inch ties and waistband, cut strips of fabric 4 inches wide (this includes 1 inch for seam allowances). Cut and piece together enough strips to measure the length of the top edge of the skirt plus enough for two ties, one twice as long as the other (say 10 inches and 20 inches), so it can wrap around your waist (Figure 114).

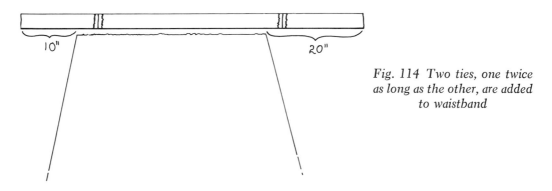

Fig. 114 Two ties, one twice as long as the other, are added to waistband

6. To give body to the waistband, cut a strip of lightweight interfacing one half the width of the band. Cut the interfacing the length of the top edge of the skirt, not including the tie length. Baste the interfacing to the wrong side of the waistband as shown. Trim away ½ inch of the interfacing along the unstitched edge (Figure 115).

94

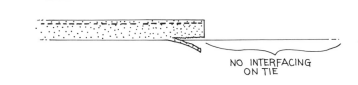

*Fig. 115 Interfacing is basted
to wrong side of waistband and
trimmed from seam allowance*

NO INTERFACING
ON TIE

7. Pin the unfolded edge of the waistband to the top of the skirt, right sides together. Position the longer tie on the left side of the skirt. Stitch the waistband (Figure 116). Trim the seam allowance.

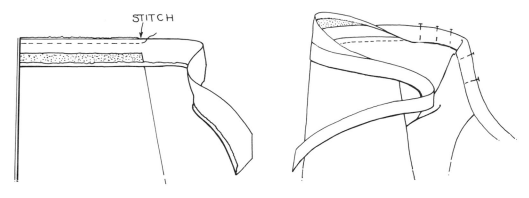

STITCH

Fig. 116 Stitching the waistband to the skirt   *Fig. 117 Folded edge of waistband is pinned
to stitching on wrong side*

8. Press the waistband in half and then press it up and away from the body of the skirt at the seam. Pin the folded edge to the stitching on the wrong side (Figure 117).

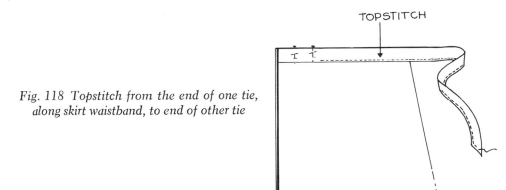

TOPSTITCH

*Fig. 118 Topstitch from the end of one tie,
along skirt waistband, to end of other tie*

9. Topstitch the waistband and ties to the skirt. Begin at the end of one tie, continue stitching along the skirt waistline and to the end of the other tie (Figure 118).

10. Try the skirt on and mark your right side by inserting a pin in the waistband. Then remove the skirt and make a buttonhole opening at the pin mark for the left tie.

95

11. To make a buttonhole opening, cut a ½-inch slash in the waistband. Then finish the raw edges of the slash, using either a tight zigzag stitch or a handmade buttonhole stitch (see Figure 132). Thread the longer tie on the left side through the buttonhole, wrap it around the back of your waist, and tie it on the left side (see Figure 123).

TOP

12. Try the top on, inside out. Pinch in and pin the underarm and side fullness, tapering at the sleeves (Figure 119).

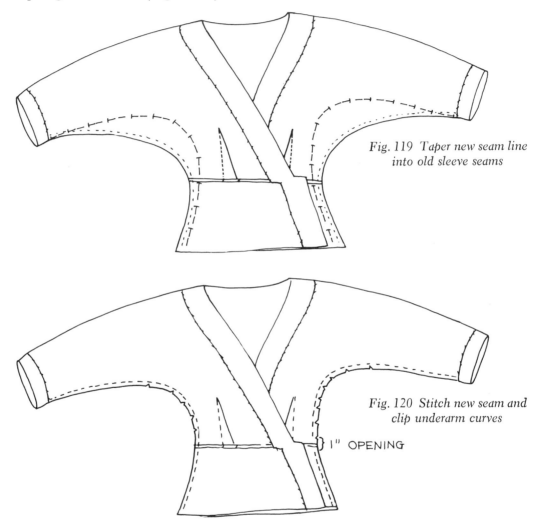

Fig. 119 Taper new seam line into old sleeve seams

Fig. 120 Stitch new seam and clip underarm curves

1" OPENING

13. Stitch on the pin line, tapering into the original seam at the sleeves. Leave a 1-inch opening for a tie at the right side of the waistline. Cut the excess from the underarm and clip the curve so it lies flat (Figure 120). Turn up the bottom edge of the peplum and sew a narrow hem.

14. Make two ties, using 1-inch-wide ribbon or excess fabric from the skirt. Decide how long you want the ties to be (say 8 inches). Cut one tie 8 inches and, because the

96

other tie will wrap halfway around your waist, cut it 8 inches plus half your waist measurement.

15. To make the ties from fabric, cut two 2½-inch-wide strips the appropriate lengths. Press the raw edges under ¼ inch and then press the ties in half lengthwise, wrong sides together. Pin and topstitch the folded ties ⅛ inch from the edge as shown in Figure 121.

Fig. 121 Fold raw edges under ¼ inch; topstitch ⅛ inch from edges

STITCH ⅛" FROM EDGE   ¼" FOLDED

16. Attach a tie to the waistline edge of each front flap. Attach the longer tie to the left flap as shown in Figure 122. When the top is wrapped closed, the left flap will go underneath and the longer tie will thread through the opening on the right, wrap around the back, and join the shorter tie at the left (Figure 123).

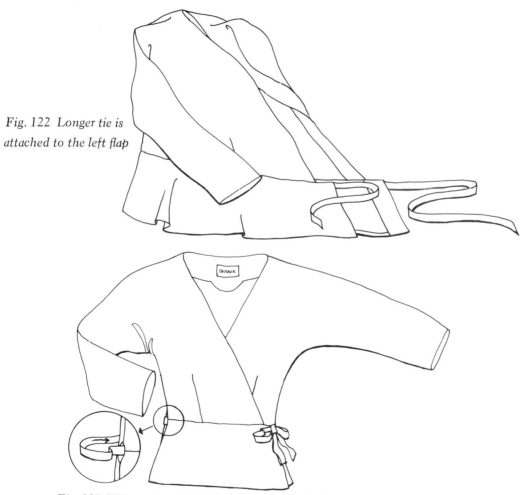

Fig. 122 Longer tie is attached to the left flap

Fig. 123 When closed, left flap goes underneath; longer tie threads through opening and around the back

97

100

101

6 /
TRANSFORMING LINGERIE AND LOUNGEWEAR INTO STREET CLOTHES

Delicate old lingerie make beautiful summer clothing. Often they were made with rich fabrics—silks, crepes, satins, or voiles—and trimmed with fine lace. Such items as petticoats and camisoles can combine to make a fragile party outfit. Or wear lacquered satin slips and nightgowns from the '30s as elegant evening dresses.

Old loungewear, bedjackets, for instance, make soft tops either worn open or tied above the waist. Wear them alone or over T-shirts with jeans or skirts. They also look comfortable over slip dresses like the combination in Figure 124.

Old lingerie or loungewear may need repairs or alterations before you can wear them; here are some sewing tips for working with sheer, delicate fabrics.

STITCHING

Use fine or ballpoint needles on delicate fabrics so they won't be damaged. Choose silk or extra-fine polyester/cotton thread. Use short stitches—14–18 per inch. When sewing on lace or other sheer, slippery fabrics, place tissue or other paper between the fabric and the machine so the fabric won't get marred or caught in the presser foot or feed dog. Then tear the paper away when you're finished stitching.

MENDING

If you need to mend old lingerie, do it with appliques of lace or other fine fabric rather than with geometric patches. To make these appliques, carefully cut out the individual designs from the lace piece. Attach them with a fine hand stitch or a machine zigzag stitch. You can connect several lace appliques with embroidery or cut out the fabric underneath the applique so your skin shows through. Or use different colored fabrics to back the sheer applique. Don't put too much handwork on delicate fabric, though, or it might weaken and tear.

If your lingerie is too sheer, dye it a darker color to help hide its transparency. To avoid an "underwear" look, sew bands of wide lace to the narrow shoulder straps.

REMODELING GUIDE
Before Beginning. Read all the instructions for a particular remodeling change first.

Fig. 124 Minor adjustments transform slip and bed jacket into evening ensemble

Trying On. Try the garment on throughout the remodeling process to make sure of the fit, especially when you're pinning new seams.

Seam Allowance. Use ½ inch seam allowance when cutting fabric or sewing.

Pressing. Press seam allowances open after sewing the seam. Press the garment completely when finished.

Backstitch. Backstitch (reverse stitch) or fasten the threads at the beginning and end of all stitching.

SLIPS AND NIGHTGOWNS

Slips and nightgowns can be worn as evening dresses or made into casual tops to wear with pants or skirts. Those from the '30s are perfect candidates because they were made like the dresses of the time, with bias cutting or gored panels and a flare at the hem for ease of movement.

Slip into Evening Dress

If a slip is too large, take in the side seams. Then make any length adjustments needed and fix the straps as explained in steps 1 and 2 of *Slip into a Top* below. Add lace edging or other trim at the bodice and hem edge or attach a fabric flower at the center front. To complete the look, wear the dress with a shawl made from an old lace tablecloth or a soft bed jacket as shown in Figure 124.

Slip into a Top

To make a slip into a top, you can cut the slip off below the waist, make a hem, and then tuck it into a long skirt or wear it out over jeans. Or cut the slip off at the waist and then add a peplum, using fabric from the bottom, keeping the lace at the edge intact so it matches the lace at the bodice (Figure 125).

1. Run the metal bars of the straps to the front. Cut the straps off at the front bodice edge and then cut the metal bars off, leaving a single strap (Figure 126).

2. Resew the straps to the underside of the front bodice edge.

3. Cut the slip in two at the waist. Pinch in the side seams if the slip is too big and pin them to fit. Cut off the excess ½ inch outside the pin line. Stitch the right side seam, but leave the left one open for a zipper.

4. Cut off a 10-inch piece from the bottom of the slip skirt and use it for a peplum.

5. Take in the side seams of the peplum to match the width of the bodice waistline. Leave the left side open 4 inches down from the top for the zipper. Seam the peplum to the bodice. Then baste the zipper opening closed.

6. Insert a 12 inch plastic zipper (it's lighter than a metal one) on the left side of the bodice. Follow the package directions for the lapped method. Sew a hook and eye to the top of the closure if needed.

7. Add small crochet pieces, embroidery stitches, or fabric flowers for added trim if you like.

Fig. 125 Slip converts easily into a peplum top

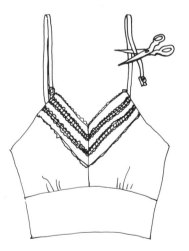

Fig. 126 Remodeling slip straps

Nightgowns into Tops

Fitted Style. Cut the nightgown off below the waist at the length you want. Take in the side seams to get a better fit and insert a lightweight plastic zipper on the left

106

side, following package instructions. Hem the bottom edge (Figure 127).

Elasticized Waistline. Cut the nightgown off at the hip line and hem. Elasticize the waistline, either all the way around or just in the back. To do this measure a narrow strip of elastic around your waist. It should fit comfortably, but not tightly. Mark your waistline on the inside of the gown with a light chalk line.

Pin the elastic to the chalk line, spacing it evenly all the way around. Sew it on with a tight zigzag stitch, stretching the elastic as you go so it lies flat against the nightgown. When you're finished the elastic will spring back, bringing the nightgown in to fit (Figure 128).

Blouson. Cut the nightgown off at the waist and create a blouson effect (Figure 129) by inserting a drawstring or an elastic band, explained in steps 3–5 of the following section.

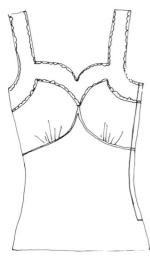

Fig. 127 Fitted top from   Fig. 128 Top with elasticized   Fig. 129 Blouson style top
      nightgown   waistline

PETTICOATS AND CAMISOLES

Petticoats and camisoles were typical turn-of-the-century underwear. Both were often elaborately trimmed with ribbons, ruffles, and cobwebby lace. They usually had intricate handwork in the form of tiny tucks and pleats, embroidery, and fabric rosettes.

Petticoat into Summer Skirt

Petticoats were usually made of nonsheer fabrics, such as cotton and linen, and frequently adorned at the bottom with layers of ruffles that had scalloped edges or lace trimmings. Today they make perfect summer skirts, but they may need some adjustments since they're often too big at the waist or too long. In the example here, the waist was drawn in with a drawstring (an elastic band could also be used and is explained below as well). To shorten it, the excess was cut off at the top to avoid cutting into the lace ruffles at the bottom (Figure 130).

107

Fig. 130 Petticoat becomes a summer skirt

1. Try the petticoat on and pull it up at the waist until the length is correct. Mark where your waistline hits the skirt with a pin.

2. Take the petticoat off, then measure the distance from the waist edge to the pin. Continue marking this length with pins all the way around. Cut 1¼ inches above the pin line. Remove the pins.

3. Make a self-casing for a drawstring or an elastic band by turning down the waistline edge 1 inch. Either hem it by hand or topstitch by machine close to the edge. (For an elastic band, leave the hem open 1 inch at the center front—see step 5 below.)

4. For a drawstring waist, stitch the hem completely closed and make two ½-inch slashes at the center front. The slashes are through the top layer of the casing only, stopping just above the hem (Figure 131).

Finish the edges of the slashes with a hand blanket stitch or a hand buttonhole stitch. The latter is made by inserting the needle and looping the thread under the needle point as shown in Figure 132. Bring the needle out over the thread and pull the loop tight. Then attach a safety pin to one end of the drawstring—thin satin or velvet ribbons are good—and work it through the casing. Tie the drawstring together at the front and gather the skirt around it.

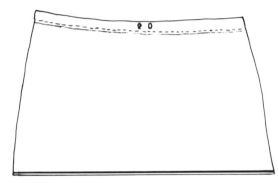
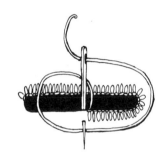

Fig. 131 *Two ½-inch slashes are made in casing at center front*

Fig. 132 *Slashes are finished with hand buttonhole stitching*

5. For an elastic band, leave the hem open 1 inch in the center front (Figure 133). Then cut a narrow piece of elastic so it fits around your waist snugly. Attach a safety pin to one end of the elastic and work it through the casing. Stitch the ends of the elastic together, then stitch the 1-inch opening closed.

Fig. 133 *Hem is left open for insertion of elastic, then closed*

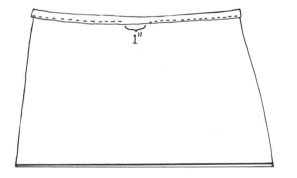

109

Duplicating Camisoles

Victorian camisoles make fragile tops. They usually have low square necks with button-down fronts, narrow shoulder straps, and lace or eyelet trim. Figure 134 shows an example of a strapless variety with a drawstring top and loose bottom. The old ones are hard to find, though, especially in good condition. But ripped trims and worn closures can be replaced and the whole thing dyed to brighten it up.

If you can't find an old camisole, make one yourself out of cotton, linen, lace, or doilies. The length of your fabric should be between 40 and 50 inches. It should be wide enough to cover you from your underarms to your waist. Finish the ends with a narrow hem and attach hooks and eyes or snaps for the closure.

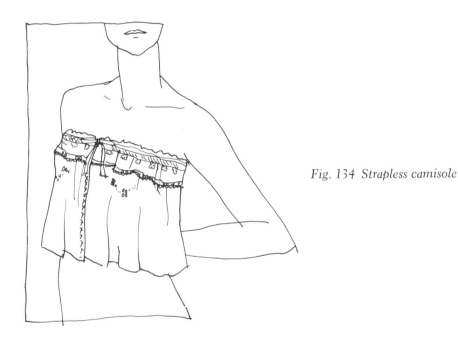

Fig. 134 Strapless camisole

Make casings for drawstrings or elastic bands on the top and bottom edges by following steps 3–5 in the preceding section. Or simply leave the bottom edge open, as shown in Figure 134. Make wide straps out of ribbon or fabric. (If you use fabric, make the straps following the instructions for fabric ties in step 15, under *Wrapped Dress into Skirt and Peplum Top*, Chapter 5.) Add lace, embroidery, or other delicate trims if you like.

ROBES AND LOUNGING PAJAMAS

Secondhand stores and antique shops often have old robes and wide-legged lounging pajamas that were made with an Oriental look. Luxurious satin or crepe fabrics were used frequently, with prints and colors of the East and details like quilting, piping, raglan sleeves, and frog closings. Sometimes you need only make a few changes to be able to wear these as great-looking street clothes.

For example, if you find a pair of lounging pajamas you can wear the top as a light jacket or elasticize the legs for a harem look. Often the pants had excessively low crotches that you may want to raise. You can do this by pulling them up at the waist so they fit. Then cut off the excess at the top and refinish the waist edge, making it fit with a drawstring, an elastic band, or by taking in the side seams. If taking the pants up like this leaves the legs a little short, cut them off just below the knee for a gaucho look or elasticize the bottom edges and wear them as knickers. Or you can even change the pants into a side-slit skirt as Laurie Hazlett did.

Fig. 135 Side-slit skirt

Wide-Legged Pajama into Side-Slit Skirt

1. Undo the inseam of the pants and fold the pants at the center front and back seams. Cut off the front and back curves that gave shape to the crotch area (see Figure 177).

2. Sew the inside edges of the front legs together and turn the pants so the seam is now at the left side. (This will move any side closure to the center back.)

3. Round the bottom edges at the sides of the other (back) legs as shown in Figure 135 and rehem them.

4. Sew these legs together as far down as you want, but leave the seam open enough for ease of movement. Wear the skirt as is or over narrow-legged lightweight pants.

Duster into Oriental Jacket

Kimono-type wrap robes can be cut off at the hipline, hemmed and worn as light jackets. Another easy way to make an Oriental jacket is from an old quilted duster robe as J.J. did here (Figure 136). It's especially effective if you can find one made of satin or some other shiny fabric.

Fig. 136 Duster transformed into Oriental style jacket

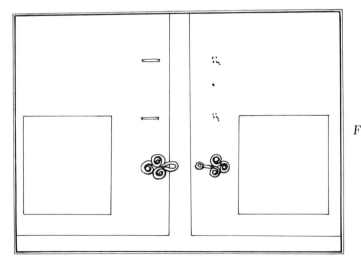

Fig. 137 Replacing old buttons with frog closures

1. Cut off the robe at the hip line and rehem it.

2. Buy Chinese frog closures at a sewing shop or notions department and use them to replace the original closures. Sew the buttonholes closed and cover them with the looped halves of the frogs. Attach the frogs from the underside with tacking or running stitches. Remove the buttons from the robe and replace them with the other halves of the frogs (Figure 137).

3. Turn the collar up and sew on snaps to hold it closed.

Kimono Robe into Pants

If you get lucky you may find an authentic old kimono robe in a thrift shop or at a swap meet. Though these robes are sometimes damaged, the fabric can be used to make something else. J.J. reworked the kimono illustrated in Figure 139 into a pair of pants. We then teamed it with the cutoff bodice of a cheongsam (an Oriental dress).

1. Get a pattern for wide-legged pants, avoiding an elasticized waist as the continual stretching can weaken and tear the delicate old fabric. Instead, use a zipper closure for a smooth fit and to eliminate strain on the fabric.

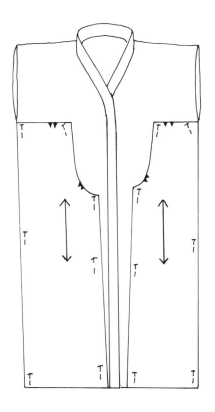

Fig. 138 Pattern pieces are positioned on the folds

Fig. 139 *Kimono made into pants, teamed with cheongsam bodice*

2. Remove the sleeves from the kimono and pin the pants pattern pieces down on the fold at the sides as shown in Figure 138. Incorporate as much of the kimono design as you can into the pants but avoid any holes or worn spots. If you can't work around the damaged areas, repair them as best you can. Check Chapter 2 for ideas. Cut out the pants.

3. If the kimono fabric is very lightweight or weak, it is best to underline or back it with silk or taffeta. This will give strength and support to the fabric. Use the pants pattern pieces to cut out the underlining. Pin the underlining pieces to the corresponding pants pieces, wrong sides together. Make sure they fit smoothly and the edges are even. Baste them together if the fabrics are slippery and hard to handle.

4. Seam the underlining pieces together. Remove any basting threads. Insert a zipper at the left side or center back. Use the package instructions for the lapped method or see the steps in Chapter 2, under *Zippers*. Hem the pants with a hand stitch.

7 /
REFITTING
AND
REDESIGNING
SWEATERS

Sweaters are popular because they're comfortable and easy to move in. The condition of old sweaters varies, though, depending on how much they were worn and how they were stored. Some may need only minor repairs because of a few moth holes or some broken yarn. Others can be transformed with a minimum of effort and a little imagination. A good example is to attach a fur collar to one of those tubular '20s sweaters that came down over the hips and wrapped at the waist. Still others may need complete remodeling. But if you have the time and energy you can pick up a stretched-out sweater for a dollar and convert it into a sleek, modern style. Here are some tips on sewing, mending, cleaning, and remodeling old sweaters.

SEWING

Supplies

Use ballpoint needles and pins, since they will separate the yarn without piercing it.
Sewing on knits requires thread with lots of stretch, such as an all-polyester thread or a cotton-polyester combination.

Stitching

Knits and sweaters need seams that have stretch so the thread won't break as you move. Some newer sewing machines have a special stretch stitch for knits which sews the seam and finishes the edge of the seam allowance at the same time. If you don't

121

have this kind of machine, use a narrow (14–18 stitches per inch) zigzag stitch. If you don't have a zigzag setting, use a straight stitch set at 12–14 stitches per inch and stretch the sweater slightly by hand as it passes under the presser foot. This will incorporate enough stretch into the seams to keep the threads from breaking. In areas of strain like the underarm you can add another row of stitches right next to the first to further prevent breakage of thread.

Mending

You may find moth-hole damage in old sweaters because most of them were made of wool. Check for these holes before buying an old sweater by holding it up to a bright light. If it's infested with holes there isn't much that can be done. But if there are only one or two small holes, they can be mended with some of the following techniques.

First pull any loose yarn ends to the wrong side and knot them securely. Sew the edges of the hole together using small overcast stitches. Use yarn as close to the color of the sweater as you can find. Try to catch all the loops of the knit in your stitching so none will pull out or drop. Match the tautness of your stitching to that of the stitching on the rest of the sweater. Also be sure to stitch beyond the hole a little to prevent further unraveling. Knot or take tiny backstitches at the beginning and end of your stitching to secure the yarn.

You may want to cover the mended areas with some form of decoration (see Chapter 3 for ideas).

Sweaters may start to unravel at a hole, a seam that wasn't finished properly, or at an area where the threads have worn thin, such as elbows, cuffs, and necklines. You may be able to rework the stitches with a crochet hook if you have a basic knowledge of knitting or crocheting.

Some other ideas are to replace damaged cuffs with the tops from socks. Or make oval reinforcement patches out of suede or corduroy for worn elbows on sporty sweaters. Or you can cut the damaged area out completely and restyle the sweater, as discussed later in this chapter.

CLEANING AND BLOCKING

There are some special things you should do when washing an old sweater. First outline its shape on paper so you can block it back to size after it's washed if need be. Then wash the sweater by hand in cool, not lukewarm or hot, water. This is because lots of old sweaters are made of wool and are susceptible to shrinkage. After rinsing, lay the sweater out flat on an absorbent towel to dry. Don't pick the sweater up by one end only—this can cause it to stretch. Instead, pick it up with both hands, distributing the weight evenly.

If the sweater has been stretched out of shape or has shrunk in the washing process, block it back to shape. Do this when it's partially dry because the fibers will have more flexibility than when it's completely dry. Place the paper outline of the sweater that you made earlier on a cushioned surface like an ironing board. Lay the sweater flat and pin the edges to the outline, easing them in or stretching them out to fit. Place the pins at right angles to the sweater. Don't overstretch the sweater so that it pulls or buckles between the pins. Instead, place the pins closer together to avoid getting a wavy look along the edges. Let the sweater dry, pinned in this manner, then press the sweater with steam.

SHRINKING

If your sweater is so stretched out of shape that you can't block the fullness back in, you can try to shrink it to fit. Shrinking can only be done if there is elasticity left in the yarns. And it is a tricky process because it has to be done gradually. If you shrink the sweater too much, the yarns may interlock and you won't be able to stretch it back out again.

Begin the shrinking by washing the sweater in cool water. Then soak it in lukewarm water, wring it out, and lay it flat. When it's dry, try it on to check the fit. If it hasn't shrunk enough, resoak it in a large pan of lukewarm water. Adjust the temperature of the tap water so it is just a few degrees warmer than the water in the pan. Then move the pan under the tap and let the water run gently into it until the two temperatures are equalized. Remove the sweater, wring it out, and let it dry. Try it on again. If it is still too big, continue in the above manner, increasing the temperature of the tap water gradually until the desired amount of shrinkage is attained.

REMODELING GUIDE

Before Beginning. Read all the instructions for a particular remodeling change first.

Trying On. Try the garment on throughout the remodeling process to make sure of the fit, especially when you're pinning new seams.

Seam Allowance. Use ½ inch seam allowance when cutting fabric or sewing.

Pressing. Press seam allowances open after sewing the seam. Press the garment completely when finished.

Backstitch. Backstitch (reverse stitch) or fasten the threads at the beginning and end of all stitching.

ALTERING AND REMODELING

Taking in Side Seams

If you don't want to try shrinking a sweater to get it to fit, you can take in the side seams. A simple way is to pinch in the fullness on the underarm and side seams as was done on the dolman-sleeved sweater illustrated in Figure 140. Then sew along the pin line and cut off the excess. You can do this on sweaters with set-in sleeves as well.

Fig. 140 Dolman-sleeved sweater can be taken in easily in under-arm and side seams

Changing a Neckline

The turtleneck of the sweater in Figure 141 started to unravel from moth-hole damage. Laurie cut off the damage and changed the turtleneck into a simple round neckline.

Fig. 141 Turtleneck into round neckline

1. Remove the ribbed turtleneck completely by cutting it off just below the neckline seam (Figure 142).

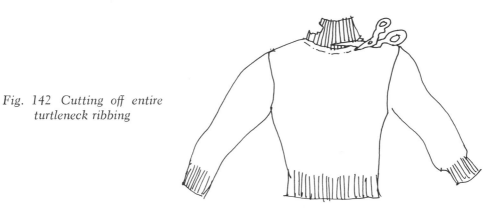

Fig. 142 Cutting off entire turtleneck ribbing

2. Cut out the damaged part of the turtleneck, as shown in Figure 143, and open it out so it lies flat.

3. Measure down 1½ inches from the top edge of the ribbing and cut across (Figure 144). Discard the bottom part or use it to replace worn cuffs on this or another sweater.

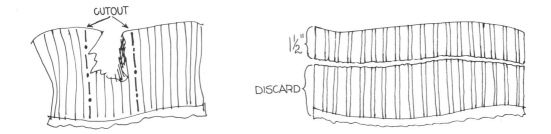

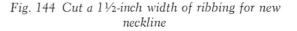

Fig. 143 Cut damaged part out of the ribbing

Fig. 144 Cut a 1½-inch width of ribbing for new neckline

4. Measure the neck opening of the sweater (for example, 20 inches) and then cut the ribbing length three quarters of that measurement (15 inches).

5. Seam the ribbing to form a circle and line the seam up with the center back of the sweater. Pin the ribbing to the neck of the sweater with right sides together, stretching it to fit as you go. Stitch.

Complete Restyling

Here's an example of a more elaborate change. Laurie took in the entire sweater and made a style change in the sleeves (Figure 145).

125

Fig. 145 Restyled and altered sweater

1. Put the sweater on, inside out. Pinch in the side seams and pin them to fit. Decide where the new armhole seams should be and mark them with pins. Mark your waistline with pins (Figure 146).

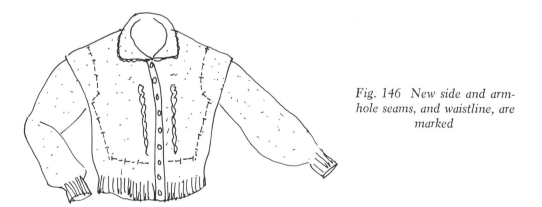

Fig. 146 New side and arm-hole seams, and waistline, are marked

2. Take the sweater off. Cut the sleeves from the armhole seams and put them aside for later. Cut off the side, armhole, and bottom excess ½ inch outside the pin lines. Be sure to maintain a proper armhole curve (see Figure 97). Cut the ribbing from the bottom piece, leaving ½ inch above it for a seam allowance.

126

3. Stitch the side seams of the sweater. Take the ribbing in at the side seams or, **if** there are none, at the center back, so it's a few inches smaller than the bottom edge of the sweater.

4. Pin the ribbing to the sweater, right sides together. Match the front openings and distribute the sweater fullness evenly along the length of the ribbing. Stitch with the ribbed side up. Gently pull the ribbing as you sew so the sweater fullness is eased in, incorporating stretch into the stitching so the thread won't break.

5. Make new sleeves from the originals you set aside earlier. Use a short, gathered sleeve pattern, adjusting it, if need be, so it will fit into the sweater armholes. Pin the pattern to the sleeves as shown and cut out the new sleeves (Figure 147).

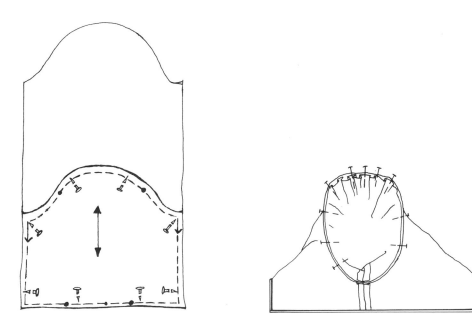

Fig. 147 *Pattern is used to cut new sleeves from old*   Fig. 148 *Working gathered sleeve into the armhole*

6. Baste the caps of the new sleeves and sew the underarm sleeve seams. With the sweater turned inside out, pin the sleeves into the armholes. Gather the sleeve caps and match the tops of them to the shoulder seams. Adjust the gathers and line up the under-arm seams of the sleeves with those of the sweater (Figure 148). Stitch with the sleeve side up so you can make sure the gathers are eased in without any tucks being made.

8 /
REWORKING
COATS
AND
JACKETS

The coats and jackets of the early decades of the century were made with a special flair. There are long fantasylike evening capes of silk velvet or richly patterned brocades . . . dolman wrap coats of the 1910s that have fur-trimmed collars, cuffs, and even hems . . . tailored cloth coats with such details as shoulder yokes and small tucks or pleats at the waist. Many of these old coats are in surprisingly good condition, but linings or fur trims are often damaged. In this section, there are instructions on how to replace a lining, some pointers on working with fur, and on replacing fur collars and cuffs. Also discussed are a couple of ways to let out turn-of-the-century dress jackets that are typically too tight.

REMODELING GUIDE

Before Beginning. Read all the instructions for a particular remodeling change first.

Trying On. Try the garment on throughout the remodeling process to make sure of the fit, especially when you're pinning new seams.

Seam Allowance. Use ½ inch seam allowance when cutting fabric or sewing.

Pressing. Press seam allowances open after sewing the seam. Press the garment completely when finished.

Backstitch. Backstitch (reverse stitch) or fasten the threads at the beginning and end of all stitching.

REPLACING LININGS

Whether the old coat you have is cloth or fur, its lining may be ripped—especially under the arms. You can fix an underarm rip by inserting a gusset, as described in Chapter 2, *Ripped Underarms*. If the lining is completely damaged, you'll have to make a new one. This isn't difficult—just follow the steps below, using fabric that is light enough in weight so it won't interfere with the hang of the coat. It should also be smooth and pliable so that it will give as you move. Silk, rayon, and taffeta are good fabrics for linings.

1. Carefully remove the original lining and undo the seams, trying not to tear any of the fabric. Mark the placement of any construction details, such as darts or tucks, with chalk.

2. Press the lining pieces so they lie flat and then use them as patterns. Fill in the missing or damaged areas when cutting out the new lining.

If the original lining is so damaged it can't be used, make a pattern on paper using the coat measurements as your guide.

3. Pin the old lining pieces onto the folded new lining fabric as shown in Figure 149. If there are duplicate pieces, such as two side fronts, cut only one. Fold the back piece in half (if it isn't already divided) and place it on the fold as shown.

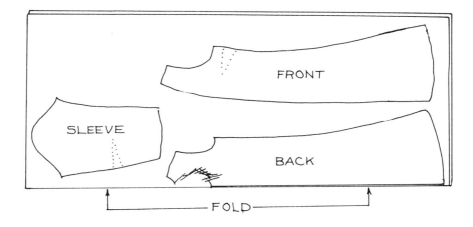

Fig. 149 Old lining pieces are pinned to new fabric

4. Cut out the lining. Make sure you cut adequate seam and hem allowances. Transfer any construction markings noted in step 1 to the new lining pieces. Sew the lining together, making any darts or tucks first, then seaming the sides and shoulders, and finally attaching the sleeves. (See Figure 101 and instructions for setting in the sleeves.) Press the lining, turning under the outer edges, and clip the neckline curve.

5. Turn the coat inside out and put it on a dress form or hanger. Pin the lining to the coat, wrong sides together, matching the seams and the center back (Figure 150).

6. Slipstitch the lining securely to the coat. Leave the bottom front edges undone a few inches and turn up the lining hem so it hangs a little above the bottom of the coat. Then hem the lining separately without attaching it to the coat (Figure 151).

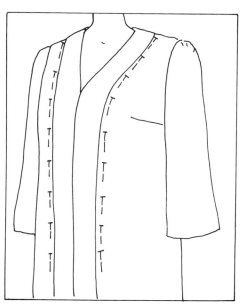

*Fig. 150 Pinning the lining to coat,
wrong sides together*

7. Match the lining sleeve to that of the coat. Bend the coat sleeve at the elbow, then move the lining up ½ inch from the edge of the coat sleeve and pin it in place. This will give more ease to the sleeve lining and keep it from being pulled and ripped when you move. Turn under the lining and attach it to the coat with a hemming stitch as shown in Figure 152.

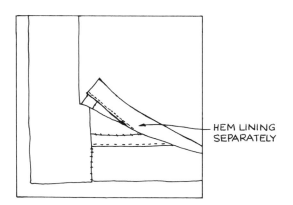

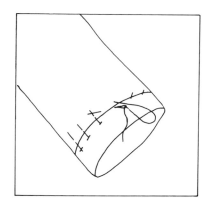

Fig. 151 Lining is hemmed separately from coat

Fig. 152 Stitching lining to sleeve cuff

WORKING WITH FUR

You can find lots of old furs ranging from full-length coats to the short "chubby" jackets popular today. There are many short-haired ones like Persian lamb, beaver, and seal; or long-haired furs like fox, mink, lynx, monkey, and raccoon. Some will be cheap, others more expensive. The price usually depends on the condition and type of fur.

Before you buy a fur, check to see if it's weak or needs repair. Pull on the seams and on the hide (fur) to see if they'll rip. Look for balding spots and matted fur that has lost its silky feel. And check the leather backing to see if it's still soft and pliable—if it's brittle it will tear easily.

If the fur has some damage, but is cheap and still looks good from the outside, you can make minor repairs that will at least get the coat through one cold winter. Major adjustments are a job for a professional, but you can try mending some minor rips yourself. Here are some guidelines.

Cutting

Do any cutting of fur from the underside. Cut through the hide only, using a razor blade cutter. Then push the fur out and away from the cut edge so the cut doesn't show on the right side.

Stitching

Sew by hand, using heavy duty thread and a coarse needle. Stitch the edges of the fur backing together from the underside with a close overcast stitch. If the leather backing is brittle and rips when you put a needle through it, use iron-on patches or fabric adhesive to mend the area.

If the coat lining is worn, replace it following directions in the preceding section. You could use a colorful, water-repellent fabric for the lining, thus making a reversible coat. And if you happen to find a stole, collar, or other small piece of fur the same as your coat, make patch pockets to attach to the reversible lining.

Cleaning and Storing

If your fur is badly soiled, you should have it professionally cleaned. If it's just musty, shake or brush it gently and hang it outside to air. Or use a small vacuum cleaner to remove loose dirt by moving it back and forth a little above the coat. Don't bend or fold a fur; hang it on a sturdy wood hanger in a cool, ventilated place. Don't seal it in a plastic bag, use a muslin one so the fur can breathe.

REPLACING FUR COLLAR AND CUFFS

The style of old cloth coats can be enhanced by adding fur collars and cuffs when there are none, or by removing the existing worn fur pieces and adding more attractive ones. There are examples of both in this section.

Follow these preliminary steps to get old fur collars and cuffs that will fit your coat. First measure around the coat cuffs and note the distance. Then make an outline of the size and shape of the coat collar on paper. Take these measurements with you when you shop for fur and buy pieces as close to the right size as you can find. You probably won't be able to find exact matches, so get pieces a little larger.

136

Fig. 153 A *few adjustments and additions transform secondhand coat*

J.J.'s Coat

The coat illustrated in Figure 153 had buttons missing, sleeves that were too short, and a boxy, drab look. J.J. added a fur collar and cuffs, replaced the buttons, and made a suspender belt to bring in the waist. The fur collar was too large for the coat, so she took it in to fit. (You could also let out the coat collar instead of cutting into the fur—see step 6, under *Cheryl's Coat.*) The fur cuffs were extended a little below the sleeve edge so they would lengthen the too-short sleeves.

1. Place the fur collar and cuffs on the coat in the position in which they will be sewn. If they're too big, mark with pins where they should be taken in.

2. Remove the fur pieces from the coat and pin in the fullness, right sides together. In this case, the cuffs were taken in with a straight seam. The collar excess was taken in with a triangular-shaped wedge so the curve of the fur would fit the coat collar (Figure 154).

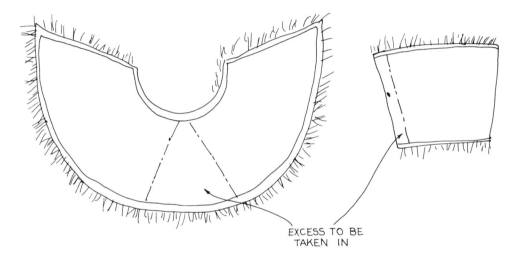

EXCESS TO BE
TAKEN IN

Fig. 154 Cuffs can be taken in with straight seam; collar is altered by seaming triangular wedge

3. Cut off the excess fur and stitch the edges together. Make similar adjustments to the fur lining, as well.

4. Pin the fur pieces to the coat. Let the bottom edge of the cuffs hang down beyond the coat sleeve if you need to add length.

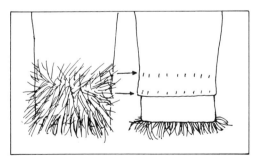

Fig. 155 Cuffs are stitched to sleeve along top edge and where bottom of coat sleeve meets cuff

5. Attach the fur pieces with a running stitch made from the underside. Catch a bit of the fur backing and a thread of the coat in each of your stitches. Stitch all edges of the fur collar to the coat.

Undo the lining at the bottom of the sleeves. Stitch each cuff to the coat at the top edge of the cuff and where the bottom of the coat sleeve meets the cuff (Figure 155). Rehem the lining.

Fig. 156 New collar and fabric belt give flair to old coat

6. Sew on new buttons to replace the missing ones. Make a belt from an old suspender, removing the metal bars and sewing an old buckle to the ends. (Some second-hand shops have unusual deco buckles.) Hook the belt around the waist to bring in the coat.

Cheryl's Coat

The coat shown in Figure 156 was updated by shortening it and adding a belt made from the excess fabric. The old damaged fur pieces were removed and a new collar added. The fur collar was too large for the coat so Cheryl let out the coat collar to get a better fit.

1. Carefully remove old fur collar and cuffs with seam ripper.

2. Try on the coat and mark the new length. Take it off and measure from the pin to bottom edge. Pin this distance all the way around.

3. Cut the excess from the coat and the lining 2 inches outside the pin line. Save the excess coat fabric. Finish the raw edge and make a hand-stitched hem. Finish the lining edge and hem it as described in *Replacing Linings*, earlier in this chapter.

4. Make a belt out of the excess fabric from the coat hem. Cut the belt as wide and long as you want it and follow the instructions in step 15, *Wrap Dress into Peplum Top*, Chapter 5, for putting it together.

5. Position the new fur collar around the cloth collar. If it's too large, undo the center back seam of the coat collar so it opens into a wide V. Fasten the threads of the seam when it has been opened up sufficiently.

6. If the front points of the fur collar don't line up with the front wrapped edges of the coat, undo the seams at the edges of the coat. Then turn the excess to the inside (if there's a lot of excess, cut it to ½ inch) and resew the seam, lining it up with the tip

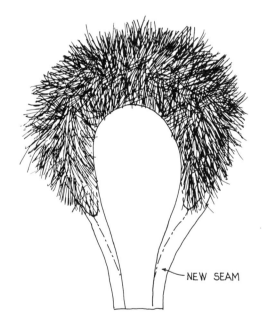

Fig. 157 *Reworking seam where collar is attached to coat*

NEW SEAM

140

of the fur collar as shown in Figure 157. Taper the new seam smoothly into the original or make a new seam all the way down.

7. Pin the collar to the coat and attach it with a running stitch from the underside.

JACKETS

Tailored '40s Styles

There are lots of tailored, square-shouldered suit jackets from the '40s. Sometimes all that's needed to liven them up is a change of shoulder pads. You'll have to undo the lining a bit at the shoulders, detach the old pads, and either buy new ones or make them yourself (see Figures 76 and 77).

Dress Jackets

Turn-of-the-century dress jackets are often too small at the waist—the ideal waist at that time was 18 inches! Whale-bone corsets helped, of course.

Fig. 158 Decorative strips of drapery trim assembled to make a snap-in panel

INSERTING CENTER FRONT PANEL

One way to enlarge a tight jacket is to insert a decorative piece in the front the way Sylvia Lane Winner did (Figure 158). She used strips of old drapery trim, stitched them together, and then sandwiched the edges between iron-on tape. The inset was then attached to the jacket with snaps.

141

Other insets could be made from old crochet or embroidered pieces, or lace dyed to match the color of the jacket.

LETTING OUT SEAMS

Here's an example of an 1890s dress jacket with a waist that's too small (Figure 159). It had many seams in the sides and back with enclosed whale-bone stays for support. Laurie found that the seam allowances were ample and so she let each out enough to make the jacket fit.

Fig. 159 1890s dress jacket had ample material in seams to let out

1. The casings that covered the stays were undone and the stays taken out (Figure 160).

2. The binding at the back waistline was removed and the waistline seam undone, as shown in Figure 161.

3. All seams were opened from the waist up, to about 2 inches before each seam ended (Figure 162).

142

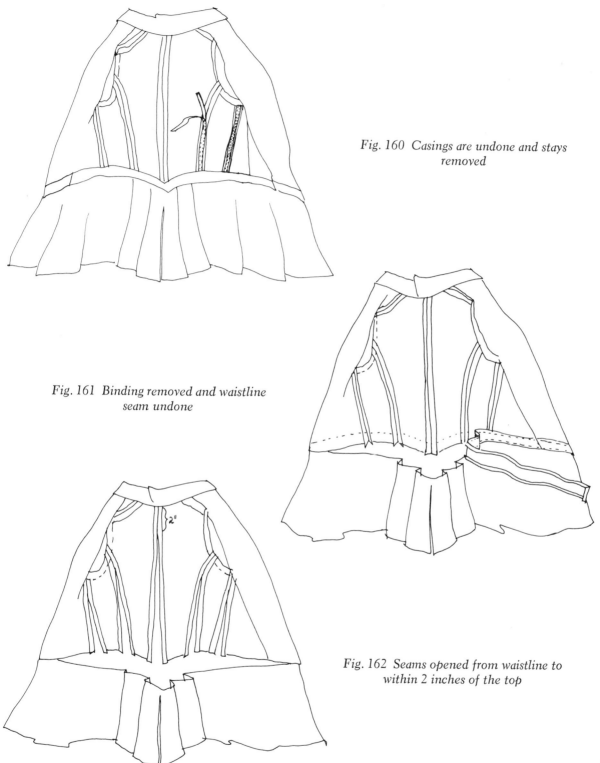

Fig. 160 Casings are undone and stays removed

Fig. 161 Binding removed and waistline seam undone

Fig. 162 Seams opened from waistline to within 2 inches of the top

143

4. The seams were resewn, using as little seam allowance as possible. They were sewn from the top of the seam to the waistline.

5. The skirt was then pinned back, and the pleats let out a little to fit the new fullness. The waistline seam was resewn. The seam allowances were finished with seam binding.

6. The new seams needed to be professionally pressed because of long-standing creases.

9 /
ALTERING
AND
UPDATING
JEANS

Old denim jeans and jackets are soft and comfortable and so popular they're being worn worldwide. Making alterations on jeans can be frustrating and time consuming, though, because of the bulkiness of the seams (often flat-felled) and the difficulty of working around those metal rivets often used to hold pockets in place. So if you plan to do any major remodeling, be sure you have sufficient time and uncommon patience.

Here are some hints to make your work easier and to help you get a more professional look.

Needle and Thread. Use size 14–18 needles on your sewing machine. These are the largest and strongest. Use an extra-strong all-purpose thread—a synthetic, cotton-synthetic blend, or mercerized cotton thread.

Stitching. Always sew by machine when remodeling denim garments because the stitching is stronger and lasts longer than hand sewing. Set your machine for 8–10 stitches per inch.

REMODELING GUIDE

Before Beginning. Read all the instructions for a particular remodeling change first.

Trying On. Try the garment on throughout the remodeling process to make sure of the fit, especially when you're pinning new seams.

Seam Allowance. Use ½ inch seam allowance when cutting fabric or sewing.

Pressing. Press seam allowances open after sewing the seam. Press the garment completely when finished.

145

Backstitch. Backstitch (reverse stitch) or fasten the threads at the beginning and end of all stitching.

SEAMS

Jeans and other denim items are often sewn with flat-felled seams. These seams are strong and will withstand lots of wear.

Flat-Felled Seam

Sew a plain seam but with the wrong sides of the fabric together, not the right sides as is normally done. Press this seam to one side and trim the underneath seam allowance to ⅛ inch. Then turn the edge of the top seam allowance under and pin it over the bottom one. Topstitch through all thicknesses close to the folded edge (Figure 163).

If you have difficulty sewing this seam because of the bulkiness of the folds, you can make a lapped seam which has only one fold. Here's how.

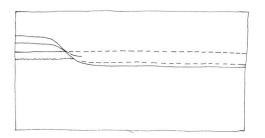

Fig. 163 Flat-felled seam

Lapped Seam

Zigzag stitch the edges of the seam allowance to prevent raveling. Working on the right side of the jeans, press the raw edge of one seam allowance under ½ inch. Overlap this folded edge over the other seam allowance ½ inch and pin. Stitch close to the folded edge through all three thicknesses (Figure 164).

Matching New and Old Seams

If you have to undo parts of seams when you're remodeling your jeans, use a sharp seam ripper or a razor blade cutter. If this takes too much time because of the strong stitching (and *if* the fit of the jeans allows), cut off the seams entirely. Then make new seams, being sure to match them to the originals for a finished look.

If you're joining a new plain seam into an old one, simply blend the new stitching line into the original. If the old seam is flat-felled, however, it will mean more work. You'll have to first undo the original seam a little beyond the remodeled area. Then clip the folds of the seam allowance and open them out so they lie flat. Cut off any excess and taper the folds and stitching of the original seam into those of the new seam.

If you have difficulty blending the flat-felled seams, make the new seam with the lapped method, described above, and add another row of topstitching the same distance away as the original flat-felled seam (Figure 165). This is easier to make and will dupli-cate the look of the flat-felled from the right side.

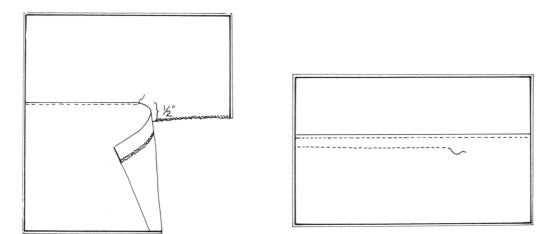

Fig. 164 Lapped seam   *Fig. 165 Matching new and old seams*

PATCHING

Old jeans often have holes or worn spots, especially at the seat and knees. A good way to cover them is to make a collage of decorative patches (Figure 166). Use strong, washable fabrics that are comparable in weight to your jeans. Good combinations are

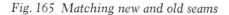

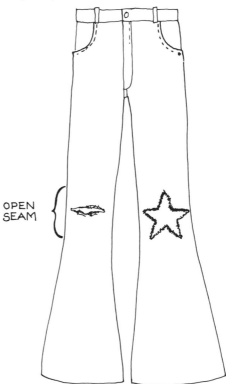

Fig. 166 Decorative patch collage camou-   *Fig. 167 Open seam makes knee more*
flages worn area   *accessible for patching*

147

faded and regular denim interspersed with drapery fabric, quilting, brocade, or corduroy. See Chapter 3 for instructions on assembling and attaching the collage.

You may have trouble getting the machine into the narrow knee area when patching your jeans. To make the job easier, undo and open the inseam or side seam as much as needed—this will give you room to work (Figure 167). Then resew the seam in the original manner when you're done patching.

ALTERING LENGTH

Shortening Legs

Basically, all that needs to be done to shorten the legs is to cut off the excess and turn under a new hem the desired amount. You should always make a narrow machine-stitched hem on jeans because it's strong and durable. A popular variation is to have the back slightly longer than the front (Figure 168).

1. Try the jeans on with the shoes you plan to wear and place a pin at the center front where the hem should be turned up. Take the jeans off and measure the distance from the bottom edge of the pants to the pin (say 3 inches).

2. In order to get the ½ inch slant in the back of the hem, measure up 2½ inches from the bottom edge of the center back and pin. Then place a pin at each side seam 2¾ inches up from the bottom edge (Figure 169).

3. Measure down 1 inch from each pin and cut off the excess. Remove the pins.

4. Press the hem to the wrong side, making two ½-inch folds. Pin the hem to the jeans, matching the side seams. Stitch by machine.

Fig. 168 *Tapered hem, longer in back*

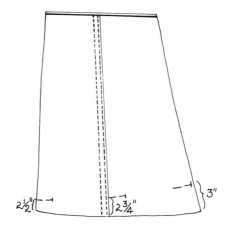

Fig. 169 *Measuring and marking for tapered hem*

Lengthening Legs with Patchwork

If your jeans are too short, you can tuck the legs into boots or wear them rolled up with textured stockings and sporty shoes. Or you can lengthen the legs by adding fabric bands or wide trim to the bottom. Then repeat the trim on the pockets or as a sash to complete the look.

Another more complicated way to lengthen jeans is to cut off the lower part of the legs entirely and replace them with longer legs made of patchwork, as Mary McCrea did here (Figure 170).

Fig. 170 Patchwork lengthens and livens old jeans

1. Try on the jeans and decide how much length needs to be added (for instance, 3 inches).

2. On the wrong side of the jeans, draw in V shapes with tailor's chalk near the knees. The points of the Vs should fall at the center front and back, as shown in Figure 171.

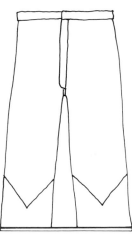

Fig. 171 V shapes are drawn with points at center front and back

149

3. Cut off the legs at the chalk lines and use one of them to make a pattern. Undo the side seam of this leg and press the seam allowance flat. (If you prefer cutting the seam allowance off rather than undoing it, add ½ inch to the side seams of the pattern.)

4. To make the pattern, place the opened leg on paper and draw around it. Add the length determined in step 1 (3 inches) plus 1 inch for a hem allowance (total 4 inches). Follow the slant of the leg so the added length flares. Add ½ inch for a seam allowance at the top of the Vs, as shown in Figure 172. Measure the total length and width of the leg pattern at its longest and widest points and cut it out (18 inches x 20 inches).

5. Make a patchwork piece of fabric for the new legs. Double the width measurement of the pattern so there is enough to cut two legs (18 inches x 40 inches) and make the patchwork this size. Assemble the piece following the instructions in Chapter 3, under *Patchwork*. Then pin the pattern onto the patchwork piece and cut out two legs.

6. Rip out the side seams on the upper part of the jeans about 9 inches. This will make it easier to sew on the patchwork legs.

7. Lap the edges of the jean Vs ½ inch over the patchwork legs, as shown in Figure 173.

8. Topstitch the edges of the jeans using a tight zigzag stitch. To reinforce it and to keep the edges from unraveling, be sure to go over the zigzag stitch at least one more time.

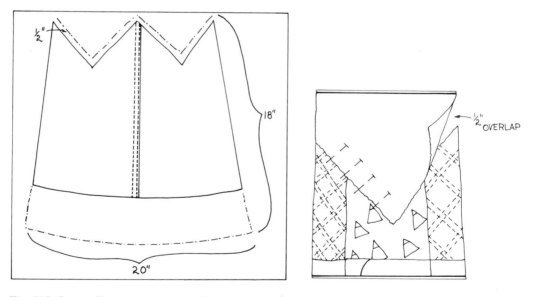

Fig. 172 *Seam allowances and extra length are added to pattern*

Fig. 173 *Attaching patchwork*

9. Pin the side seams together. Stitch, blending the original seams into the seams of the patchwork legs as explained earlier in this chapter.

10. Hem the legs, using a zigzag stitch to complement the stitching at the Vs. Press the patchwork legs well, making a crease where the inseam should be.

150

JEANS INTO COLLAGE SKIRT

Mary McCrea also lengthens jeans by cutting off the legs and making a skirt out of a collage of appliques, as shown in Figure 174. This is similar to the patchwork legs just described.

1. Cut the legs off the jeans at an angle, as shown in Figure 175.

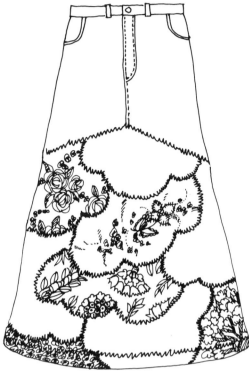

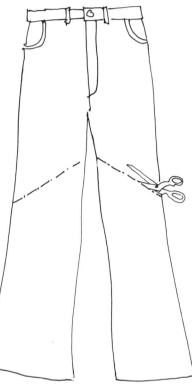

Fig. 174 Collage skirt from jeans

Fig. 175 Legs are cut off at an angle

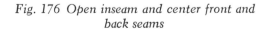

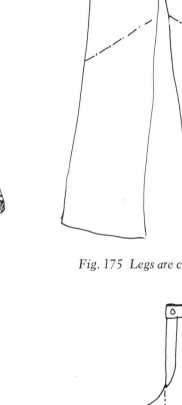

Fig. 176 Open inseam and center front and
back seams

Fig. 177 Fold and cut off curves that shape
crotch

151

2. Open the inseam. Then open the center front seam to the bottom of the zipper and open the center back seam the same distance (Figure 176). Fold the jeans at the center front and back seams and cut off the curves that gave shape to the crotch area (Figure 177).

3. Seam the front legs together from the bottom of the zipper to the cutoff edge. Do the same for the back legs.

4. Make a pattern for the bottom of an A-line skirt by laying the jeans out on a large piece of paper. Draw in lines to form the skirt, making it as wide and long as desired (Figure 178). Add ½ inch to the top edge and 1 inch to the bottom for seam and hem allowances.

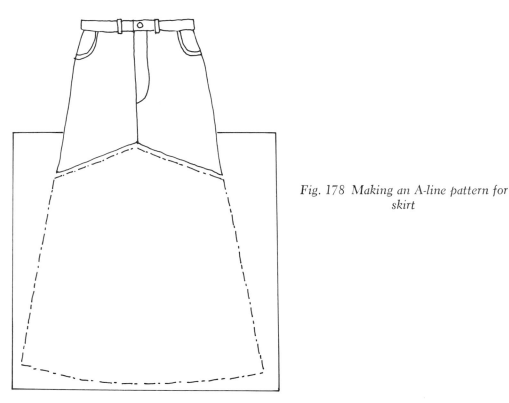

Fig. 178 Making an A-line pattern for skirt

5. To make the skirt fabric, cut out different shaped appliques from a variety of old fabrics. Then lap them together so they form a collage a little larger than your skirt pattern. Stitch the collage together, following the directions in Chaper 3, under *Collage*.

6. Place the pattern on the collage piece and cut out the skirt. Sew up the side seams of the skirt, then lap and pin the skirt over the top of the jeans. Topstitch with a tight zigzag stitch and hem the bottom edge.

REMODELING WITH GODETS

Old jeans were often made with narrow legs. One good way to widen them is to insert triangular pieces of contrasting fabric called godets. These can be inserted at the side seams (Figure 179)—or they can be inserted at the front and back seams, converting the jeans into a skirt (see Figure 183).

Widening Legs

1. Try the jeans on and decide how much width to add (say 6 inches).

2. Take the jeans off and undo the side seams from the knee down. Backstitch the seams at the knee so the stitching doesn't come undone.

3. Undo the hem a few inches to either side of the seam opening. Measure the length of the opening from the top point to the raw edge at the bottom (15 inches), as shown in Figure 180.

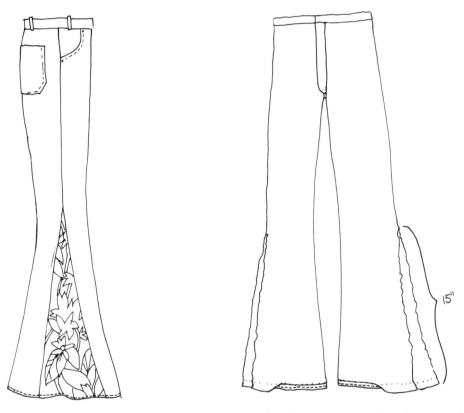

Fig. 179 *Godets convert narrow legs to flared*   Fig. 180 *Seams are opened and measured*

4. Cut a triangular piece out of fabric comparable to the weight of the jeans. Cut the length 15 inches plus 1 inch for the hem (total 16 inches). Cut the width 6 inches plus 1 inch for seam allowances (total 7 inches), as shown in Figure 181.

5. Pin the godets to the side seams of the jeans, right sides together. Stitch, starting at the bottom of one side and working to the point. Do the same on the other side. Clip the seam allowances above the point of the godet so they lie flat (Figure 182).

6. Hem the jeans and the godet with a machine stitch.

153

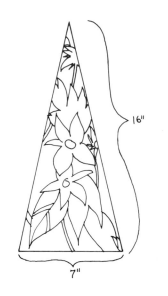

Fig. 181 Cutting the godet

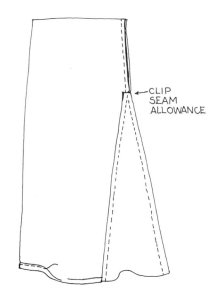
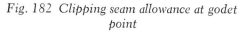

CLIP
SEAM
ALLOWANCE

Fig. 182 Clipping seam allowance at godet
point

Making a Skirt

Instead of inserting the godets at the sides of the jeans, you can put them in the front and back seams, converting the jeans into a skirt, as shown in Figure 183.

Fig. 183 Front and back godet panels
convert jeans into skirt

First open the inseams of the jeans. Then open the center front seam to the bottom of the zipper and the center back seam the same distance. Cut off the curves that gave shape to the crotch area (see Figure 177). Then restitch the center front and back seams. Cut out the godets the desired size and attach them to the front and back following steps 5 and 6 for inserting godets in legs.

TAKING IN WAISTLINES

There are several ways to take in a large waistline. You can take in the side seams or make two darts on either side of the center back if there is no back yoke—if there is one, it will be very difficult to stitch over the thick yoke seam. See Figure 93 for making darts. Or you can take in the center back seam, as explained below. If your jeans have back pockets, this method will only work if the excess is 3 inches or less. Any more than that and the pockets will be brought in too far and will start to overlap.

1. Try jeans on and measure amount of excess to be taken in (3 inches). Taper the excess down the center back and mark where the fullness ends with a pin.

2. Remove the center back belt loop on the waistband if there is one. Undo the waistband seam about 3 inches on both sides of the center back seam (total of 6 inches). Cut the waistband in two at the center back.

3. Turn the jeans inside out and mark off 1½ inches on each side of the center back seam with tailor's chalk. Connect these points to the pin that marks the end of the fullness (from step 1) by drawing in chalk lines (Figure 184). Remove the pin.

4. Cut off the excess ½ inch inside the chalk line, as shown in Figure 185.

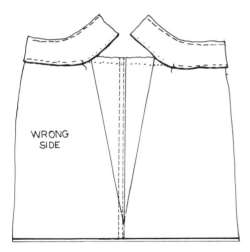

Fig. 184 *Marking off new seam*

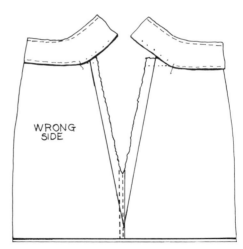

Fig. 185 *Excess fabric cut off*

5. Make a seam where you've cut off the excess, matching the original seam construction as explained earlier in this chapter, under *Matching New and Old Seams.*

6. Cut off 1¼ inches from each side of the cut waistband, as shown in Figure 186.

7. Open the folded band so it lies flat and lap one end over the other ¼ inch.

Topstitch the raw edge of the overlap with a tight zigzag stitch. Double the stitching to completely cover the raw edge (Figure 187).

8. Refold the waistband. Sandwich the waist edge of the jeans between the waistband and pin. Restitch the waistband to the jeans, following the original stitching line.

 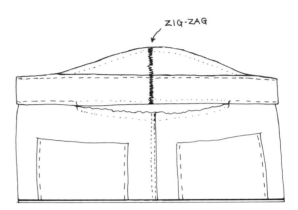

Fig. 186 *Waistband trimmed*   Fig. 187 *Double stitch the opened-out waistband*

MARY'S DENIM JACKET

It's hard to find denim jackets small enough to fit well. If you have one of the larger men's jackets, here's a way of taking it in and restyling it at the same time (Figure 188).

1. Cut off the sleeves and save them. Mark where the new armhole should be with pins. Cut off the excess ½ inch outside the pin line (see Figures 97 and 98).

2. Pinch in the side seams and pin them to fit. Stitch them on the pin line and cut off the excess.

3. Detach the waistband from the jacket and cut the bottom off to the desired length.

4. Take in the waistband to match the amount taken in on the side seams. Or make a new waistband out of old drapery fabric or brocade and extend the ends to form a tie as shown in Figure 188.

5. Make new full sleeves out of contrasting fabric. Use a sleeve pattern whose sleeve cap will fit into the jacket armhole. Insert the sleeves, following the directions in step 7, under *Bodices*, Chapter 5.

6. Undo the cuffs from the original denim sleeves. Sandwich the edge of the new sleeve between the two edges of the cuff. If the sleeve is narrower than the cuff, take the cuff in; if the sleeve is fuller, gather it to fit the cuff. Topstitch the cuff to the sleeve.

7. Decorate the jacket with lace, crochet, fabric pieces, or embroidery if you like.

Fig. 188 Baggy denim jacket restyled

PHOTOGRAPHS

USEFUL BOOKS

The instructions in this book were written on the assumption that you already have some knowledge of sewing. Here's a list of good references that'll help you learn the basics, freshen your skills in case you've gotten rusty, and stimulate your creative ideas.

BASIC SEWING

Hollis, Nesta. *Successful Sewing*. Ballantine Books, 1971.

Rosenberg, Sharon and Wiener, Joan. *The Illustrated Hassle-Free Make Your Own Clothes Book*. Bantam Books, 1972.

Schewbke, Phyllis W. and Krohn, Margaret B. *How To Sew Leather, Suede, Fur*, Revised Edition. The Bruce Publishing Company, 1970.

Simplicity Sewing Book, Revised Edition. Simplicity Pattern Co., 1973.

The Vogue Sewing Book, Revised Edition. Vogue Patterns, 1973.

FASHION DICTIONARY

Pickens, Mary Brooks. *The Fashion Dictionary: Fabric, Sewing, and Apparel As Expressed in the Language of Fashion*, Revised and Enlarged. Funk and Wagnalls, 1973.

CREATIVE SEWING IDEAS

Brock, Delia and Bodger, Lorraine. *Gladrags: Redesigning, Remaking, Refitting All Your Old Clothes*. Simon and Schuster, 1974.

Callenbach, Ernest. "Clothing," in *Living Poor With Style*. Bantam Books, 1972.

Harlow, Eve. *The Jeans Scene*. Drake Publishers, 1973.

Jacopetti, Alexandra. *Native Funk and Flash: An Emerging Folk Art*. Scrimshaw Press, 1974.

Johnson, Jann. *The Jeans Book*. Ballantine Books, 1972.

Laury, Jean Ray and Aiken, Joyce. *Creating Body Coverings*. Van Nostrand Reinhold Company, 1973.

Owens, Richard and Lane, Tony. *American Denim*. Harry N. Abrams and Warner Paperback Library.

Torbet, Laura. *Clothing Liberation, or Out of the Closets and Into the Streets*. Ballantine Books, 1973.

Waller, Jane, ed. *A Stitch in Time: Knitting and Crochet Patterns of the 1920s, 1930s, and 1940s*, Abridged Edition. Chilton Book Co., 1973.

Wolman, Baron. *Levi's Denim Art Contest Catalogue of Winners*. Squarebooks, 1974.

Useful Books

COSTUME HISTORY

Battersby, Martin. *The Decorative Thirties.* Walker, 1971.
Boucher, Francois. *20,000 Years of Fashion.* Harry N. Abrams, 1967.
Broby-Johansen, R. *Body and Clothes.* Reinhold Book Co., 1968.
Gernsheim, Alison. *Fashion and Reality 1840–1914.* Faber, 1963.
Laver, James. *The Concise History of Costume and Fashion.* Abrams, 1969.
Laver, James. *Costume Through the Ages.* Simon, 1963.
Laver, James. *Women's Dress in the Jazz Age.* Hamilton, 1964.
Lynam, Ruth, ed. *Couture, An Illustrated History of the Great Paris Designers and Their Creations.* Doubleday and Co., 1972.

TEXTILES

Arnold, Janet. *A Handbook of Costume.* Macmillan, 1973.
Joseph, Marjory L. *Introductory Textile Science.* Holt, Rinehart, and Winston, Inc., 1972.
Leene, J. E., ed. *Textile Conservation.* Smithsonian Institution, 1972.
Textile Handbook, Fourth Edition. American Home Economics Association, 1970.

NATURAL DYES

Adrosko, Rita J. *Natural Dyes and Home Dyeing.* Dover Publications, 1971.
Meyer, Clarence. "Easy Method of Dyeing Fabrics with Botanicals," in *The Herbalist.* Tenth Printing, 1973.

HERBAL POTPOURRIS

Rose, Jean. *Herbs and Things.* Grosset & Dunlap, 1972.

INDEX

Page numbers in *italics* indicate information found in illustrations